GRACE-FILLED
Motherhood

INSPIRATIONAL DEVOTIONS FOR MOMS
TO STRENGTHEN THEIR FAITH AS THEY
PURSUE THEIR PURPOSE IN CHRIST

by

AMY B. CROWE

Endorsements

"I wish Amy's book had been available when I first became a mom. Her words will not only encourage moms in all seasons of the parenting journey but help them to seek God first in each high and low. I know her words will be a gift to any mom who needs the gentle guidance of someone who is a little further along in the journey."

Abby McDonald
author of *Shift*, editor, writing coach,
and contributor for *Proverbs 31 Ministries*

"What do moms need from other moms? They need kind words of affirmation and understanding, time-tested wisdom from the trenches, a safe place to shed some tears, and inspiration to laugh together. Amy Crowe offers moms all of this, plus practical encouragement from God's Word, in *Grace-Filled Motherhood*. The short devotions will fit into a busy mom's schedule, and they offer thoughtful tidbits to ponder throughout the day. It's a perfect devotional for a mom who needs a lift."

Sarah Geringer
Creative coach, book launch manager, editor, artist,
and author of multiple books, including
Hope for the Hard Days: 100 Encouraging Devotions

"The days of motherhood are long. We give everything we have and expect very little in return. As our children grow, our roles as moms begin to shift from caregiver to coach, to mentor, to companion. We often are left dry and weary, in need of the Lord's supernatural strength to get us through.

As a fellow mom of three, I know just how essential getting daily time with God is to sustain me in my parenting. *Grace-filled Motherhood* is a beautiful and uplifting devotional that speaks directly to the hearts of mothers in every season. With heartfelt reflections and encouraging truths, it reminds moms that you don't have to be perfect to be the mother your children need—you just need to lean on the One who is. Each page offers a gentle reminder of God's grace, providing strength for the weary and peace for the overwhelmed. This devotional is a gift to every mom who desires to grow closer to God while navigating the joys and challenges of motherhood."

Morgan A. Ellis
Mom of three and author of
Rest for the Weary Mama:
Words of Hope and Encouragement
for the Worn-Out Mom

"*Grace-Filled Motherhood* is an inspiring devotional that will give you a connection point to a mom who has been there. Amy shares from experience as a mother of three who has walked through variant seasons of motherhood. The devotional encourages the reader to remain rooted in her identity as a daughter of Christ through the ever-changing seasons of motherhood and life."

Alexandra Jensen
Author of *A Place of Grace for Moms of Littles,*
Mother of three

"Amy Crowe openly shares the real, unfiltered moments of motherhood with warmth and authenticity. Within every devotion of *Grace-Filled Motherhood*, she draws from her personal journey, including her challenges and triumphs, to offer encouragement and wisdom. Every mom could benefit from the biblical insight and constant support Amy's words offer. Rich in honesty, direction, and the clear truth of scripture, Amy inspires every mother with the reassuring message – you are enough, and God will daily give you everything you need."

Lance Pate
Executive Pastor
First Baptist Church
Trussville, Alabama

"*Grace-Filled Motherhood* is a wonderful resource for moms who are feeling worn out. In our increasingly busy world, Amy offers uplifting encouragement to help moms slow down, invest in their spiritual growth, and deepen their relationship with Christ. With thoughtful insights on various aspects of parenting, Amy inspires moms to persist with hope and dedication in the rewarding journey of raising children."

Matt Galloway
Children's Minister
First Baptist Church
Trussville, Alabama

©2024 by Amy B. Crowe

Published by hope*books
2217 Matthews Township Pkwy
Suite D302
Matthews, NC 28105
www.hopebooks.com

hope*books is a division of hope*media

Printed in the United States of America

First paperback edition.

Paperback ISBN: 979-8-89185-126-9
Hardcover ISBN: 979-8-89185-127-6
Ebook ISBN: 979-8-89185-128-3
Library of Congress Number: 2024948853

hope*books
hopebooks.com
*Because the world needs your hope-filled
words now more than ever.*

This book would not be out in the world without some very special people in my life. I am so grateful to my husband for believing in me and being behind me every step of the way. You encourage my dreams and help me make them a reality. I could not have done this without you by my side.

I would like to thank my parents for their love and support, especially my mom, for her never-ending love no matter what stage I was going through. You have given me the greatest example of grace-filled motherhood, and I'm blessed to be your daughter. You mean the world to me and helped me to become the mom I am today.

Thank you to my children, who are such a blessing in my life. Being your mom is the highest privilege I could ask for, and it brings me immeasurable joy to watch you grow into who God wants you to be.

Thank you to my heavenly father, who has been my source of strength and hope through every step of motherhood and continues to bless me with new joys every day.

Table of Contents

CHAPTER 4: DIRECTION

CHAPTER 5: WISDOM

CHAPTER 6: GOD'S WILL

CHAPTER 7: FAITH

CHAPTER 8: EXAMPLE

CHAPTER 9: FRIENDSHIP

CHAPTER 10: PEACE

Introduction

Dear Mom,

If you are worn out, weary, exhausted, and just have a few minutes to spare (Ha! Ha!), I encourage you to read this devotional. This comes from the perspective of a weary and exhausted mother who needed encouragement and inspiration and, honestly, a moment for God to reveal her purpose. Being a mom is tough. Those sweet hugs are precious if you have little ones but are sometimes too exhausted to appreciate them. If your kids are tweens, they already feel sure of themselves, and those hugs are less frequent. If you have teens, a side hug, never in public, is about all you get, and by the time they are seniors and college-bound, just wave from a distance.

With three children, the struggle is real, and many days, I feel down and discouraged because I don't feel as needed as I did when they were younger. After twenty-two years of first-hand perspective of the different roles of motherhood and how they change as our children grow, I wanted to share encouragement that can help you on those tough days when you question your purpose. As children go from needing constant attention to pursuing their independence, we struggle as moms with what our role is. These devotions will not only provide perspective throughout the different stages but will also encourage you in your faith, give you ways to conquer fear, help you seek direction when you are lost, learn to hear

God's voice as you seek His will, and show you how to have peace even in the middle of chaos.

Motherhood is a joy and can be rewarding but sometimes frustrating. I knew I needed a devotional to help and encourage me in my spiritual journey. There are things I am so glad I did when they were younger, but there are things I wish I had done better, and I hope to share insight to help you learn from my mistakes.

Whatever phase you are in, please know that what you do is crucial in your children's lives. You matter. You are vital in using everyday events to teach lessons and draw them closer to Christ. No matter how old your child is, they never are too old or young to hear the love of Christ and see it in action through you.

I pray you are encouraged and uplifted and know that you have a purpose and a calling on this earth to point your kids to Christ, whether they are 2 or 22. I pray God will use this devotional to strengthen and encourage you as you strive to be the Godly mom your children need. You are not alone. Don't let another minute of your precious time go by without getting the encouragement and strength you need. We, as moms, need to join each other on this path and pursue our purpose one step at a time.

In His Love,

Amy

Encouragement

"Motherhood isn't something that just happens to you... it's a choice you make every day to put someone else's happiness and well-being ahead of your own, to teach the hard lessons, to do the right thing even when you're not sure what the right thing is... and to forgive yourself, over and over again, for doing everything wrong."
–Donna Ball

Hideouts Are a Haven

"The Lord is a refuge for the oppressed, a stronghold in times of trouble. Those who know your name trust in you for you, Lord, have never forsaken those who seek you."
Psalm 9:9-10

Have you ever tried to hide from your kids? Am I the only one? It is extremely hard, if not impossible. They will find you no matter where you go. Sometimes, as moms, we have moments where we are completely spent and exhausted. We run on empty and pressure ourselves to do one more thing because little people are counting on us. Those "little people" can be 2, 12, or 22 because when you are a mom, you are always needed. We are pulled in so many different directions, and sometimes, we need a refuge. We need to feel safe and sheltered from all the world throws at us daily.

I encourage you to find your refuge. Run to Jesus, if only for little moments throughout your day, and let him shelter you for a minute so you can get through one day at a time. Every stage is different, and your refuge times and places will change. Some of you have "little people" who take naps, and you can take just a few minutes to grab time with Christ while your littles are sleeping. Others of you may have to grab "refuge" while

3

driving down the road, in the carline, or waiting for one of yours at practice.

Trust me when I say that when you take refuge in Jesus and seek to "hide out" with him, even for a few minutes each day, you will have a better perspective as a mom. Pray while you are cleaning, turn on Christian songs in your car and even at home, and just let them play. Take Scriptures of encouragement and tape them on your fridge or mirror so you can see them daily. Work out carpool times with other mom friends to give yourself breathing room. You play a crucial role in your children's lives. To fulfill this role and become who God has called you to be, you need to consistently seek refuge and support.

Moment to Reflect:

- ♥ Am I making time to recharge myself each day?
- ♥ How can I incorporate Jesus into my day to give me strength when I need it?
- ♥ Am I trying to do too much on my own and wearing myself down?
- ♥ What can I let go of to find time to spend with Jesus?

Carefully look at each of these questions and incorporate Christian songs in your home and car, prayer time in the car or in your hiding place, place Scriptures in important main places in your home, and ask for help when you are overwhelmed.

Father, you are my hiding place, and I pray you will help me make time to run to you when I am scared and weary. You have given me the greatest and most important job, and I want to be the best I can be. Help me find refuge in you so I can take care of the ones you have entrusted to me. Lift me up and give me strength to take one day at a time. Thank you for always being there when I need you. Amen.

DAY TWO

Hold My Hand

---

*"The Lord makes firm the steps of the one who delights in Him; though he may stumble,
he will not fall, for the Lord upholds him with his hand."
Psalm 37:23-24*

How many times has your child grabbed hold of your hand for support? As infants, they reach out and learn to grasp a finger. As toddlers, they reach out as they learn to walk. As they continue to grow, they need reassurance that we are there, ready to steady them when unsure. As moms, we need our Heavenly Father's hand to steady us when we stumble. We need Him to reach out when we are struggling so we will not fall. You are never too old to need your Father's hand to steady you. Peter needed Jesus in Matthew 14:22-33 when he got out of the boat and started walking on the water. He started looking around at all that was going on around him, and when he took his eyes off Jesus, he started to sink. He lost his focus. He cried out to Jesus, and Jesus saved him.

As a mom, I've learned that during challenging times with my children, regardless of their age or stage, I need a source of strength to rely on. Jesus can be that steadfast rock when we face struggles. Each of my kids has experienced times when they desperately wanted something—whether it was an award, a spot on a particular team, or involvement in a specific activity—and didn't achieve it. Watching our children strive for something and face disappointment is incredibly hard as a parent. We wish we could shield them from their pain, and we ourselves need support during these times, as their hurt becomes our own. In these moments, I have turned to Jesus for comfort and guidance, and I encourage my children to do the same. Often, as we look back on these disappointments, we can see how they were actually blessings in disguise, helping us grow and understand God's plan.

Jesus is not only there for us Himself, but He also sends mentors into our lives who have already been through the stage we are in now. You need a mentor you trust and admire to call on when going through hard times with your kids. It could be a neighbor you trust, someone you know from church, or a mom from your child's sports team or dance/cheer team who has a child a few years older than yours. Look for a God-fearing woman who prays consistently and intercedes daily for her kids. She would also strive to broaden her family's faith and encourage her home to be centered on Christ. She would be kind to others and have integrity, raise her kids to cherish God's word, and make the most of her time and resources. My mom has been a great mentor to me because she has many of these characteristics. A mentor never takes the place of Jesus in our lives. They simply help to point us to Him when we are struggling. Jesus is the ultimate mentor we should delight in. When we delight in Him, we make time to pray to Him and thank Him for our blessings, tell Him our struggles, and ask Him for direction. I fall when I try to do things on my own and don't take hold of Jesus, who is waiting to guide me and keep me from falling.

I encourage you to delight in Him. You can do that by strengthening your relationship with Him, just like you would with a friend you haven't seen in a while. Make time for

Him, talk to Him, and tell him your fears, hurts, and dreams. Listen as he speaks to you, sometimes in His quiet whisper and sometimes through other people, songs, or Scripture. He doesn't want us to fall, but it is hard for Him to catch us when we don't reach for Him.

Moment to Reflect:

- ♥ Do I make time to talk to Jesus each day?
- ♥ Do I listen to see what He has to say to me?
- ♥ Am I frustrated with Him when I have not reached out for Him to steady me?
- ♥ What can I change to make time for Jesus like I would an old friend?

Carefully consider each of these questions and remain open to both speaking with Jesus and hearing His guidance each day. If you find yourself frustrated by setbacks, be sure to reach out and take His hand, which is always there to steady you.

Father, you never want me to fall. Your hand is always reaching out to steady me, just like I steady my own children. Help me to make time to tell you my struggles and listen for your gentle answers that will make my steps firm. Help me to reach out and grab hold so that even when I stumble, I will not fall. Amen.

DAY THREE

Count To Three

"The Lord your God is with you, the Mighty Warrior who saves. He will take great delight in you; in his love he will no longer rebuke you, but will rejoice over you with singing."
Zephaniah 3:17

There is probably no mom reading this title who didn't visualize their parents counting to three when they were younger. We count so that our child will have time to change his/her behavior, which will help us calm down a little. When I read the verse for today, my favorite part was that He will quiet you with his love. I see God counting to three to give us time to change our behavior or calm down a little.

When we get frustrated, angry, or scared about a situation, God quiets us with His love. He calms us. He allows us to take a breath.

Not only does he quiet us, but He is with us. Always. You may be going through a tough time with your child right now and wondering where God is. Sometimes, it is not until we get through something that we realize He was right there the entire time. Sadly, sometimes, we do not reach out to Him except when things get bad.

There was a time when, as a stay-at-home mom, my youngest child went to kindergarten, and I felt lost. I was used to taking care of kids all day and I didn't know what to do without one at home to take care of. I poured myself into executive board positions on PTO, room mom for multiple kids, helping with the yearbook, field trips, fundraisers, and teaching Sunday School, in addition to all the extracurricular activities I ran the kids to after school until I was completely consumed. I worked so hard trying to prove I still made a difference that I ended up in the hospital! I realized I wasn't giving God time to delight in me because I was filling my time with endless activities. There is a passage in Luke 10:38-42 that contains the story of Mary and Martha. Martha was too busy running around making sure everything was perfect and that all her lists were checked, while her sister Mary tuned out any distractions and sat at the feet of Jesus. I want to be more like Mary in my life. I don't want to be so busy with other things that I miss what is truly important. I can be a better mom when I make Jesus a priority in my life.

My husband made me keep my hospital bracelet to remind myself to slow down and make time for God so I wouldn't replace Him with endless time-consuming activities that didn't help me delight in Him. When I gave up a few of the many projects I was involved in, it freed me up to spend more time with God and listen to what He wanted me to do. He wanted me to write a children's book. That book led to a second children's book, which eventually led to this book!

Hard times drew me closer to God and forced me to realize I needed Him. We always need Him but tend to take Him for granted until we realize He is the only one who can help. We will all go through different times when we need Him more. The times I have had the hardest trials have been my greatest times of faith and, honestly, the times when I have been closer to Him.

He also delights in us and rejoices over us. He created us to fellowship with Him, and it is amazing to me that the God of the universe takes delight in me. It is encouraging to me that He gave us these Scriptures from Zephaniah so we can know that He is with us and he delights in us.

I challenge you to think of Him the next time *you* count to three. If your kids are older, maybe it's the next time you are in a store and see a parent counting to their child. We have all seen it. Just smile and thank Him for quieting us with His love.

Moment to Reflect:

- ♥ When I am going through a hard time, do I realize God is with me?
- ♥ How does knowing God is with you change your approach and your mindset about your day?
- ♥ Do I stop and try to change my behavior as he quiets me with his love?
- ♥ Does my faith get stronger when I am going through tough times?
- ♥ Have I thanked Him lately for delighting and rejoicing in me?

When you give your kids time to think about their behavior, make sure you are thinking about yours. Thank God for being with you and delighting in you and, most of all, for quieting you in His love.

Father, you count to three more times than I care to count for me. Thank you for quieting me in your love, for being there for me when I am struggling, and for delighting in me. Help me to use the quiet times in your love to think about my behavior and make sure I am being who you have called me to be. Amen.

Cry To Jesus

*"The Lord is close to the brokenhearted and saves
those who are crushed in spirit."*
Psalm 34:18

I f you are a mom, you will cling to this verse several times throughout your life. Our hearts are worn outside our bodies when we have children. Sometimes, our children may hurt us, and they do not even realize they did anything. A careless word or gesture can crush our spirit and have us holding back tears for days. When our children are younger, they don't realize they may have hurt us, but as they grow, they tend to do things intentionally, and it is extremely painful. I have had many days when I left their school crying, cried in the car, cried at home, called my husband, called my mom, and, as a last resort, cried out to Jesus.

Why do we save Him for last? There is an entire verse telling us He is close to the brokenhearted, yet we call and talk to everyone else. He saves those who are crushed in spirit, but we don't call out to Him with our hurts. Why?

God, of all people, knows what it feels like to be brokenhearted. He understands the pain of exclusion, ridicule, betrayal, suffering, watching a child hurt, and losing a child.

Kids aren't the only ones to exclude others; sometimes, moms can be the worst. Groups get formed, and sometimes, instead of opening the circle to allow one more in, we keep it tight with the ones we are comfortable with while a brokenhearted mom sits on the outside wondering what she did wrong. Many of you may have experienced betrayal by someone you love, and you are broken. Some of you have had to endure seeing your child hurt and unable to play the sport they love or reach the goals they want to reach. God is still there for you. My parents lost a child to cancer and had to watch her suffer as the disease advanced through her body and eventually took her life. God is close to the brokenhearted because he has been where we are. He weeps when we weep and wants to hold us close when we hurt. Isaiah 53:5 talks about God's son, Jesus, being pierced for our transgressions. He was beaten, mocked, and hung on a cross to save us. He took the punishment meant for us so we could have the peace of eternal life. God loves us so much that He gave His son to die for us.

If your spirit is crushed today and you feel overwhelmed and completely brokenhearted, ask Jesus to wrap you in His arms and love you through it. The hurt may not go away automatically, but when you reach out to Him, He meets you where you are and helps you conquer heartache together.

Moment to Reflect:

- ♥ Am I trying to go through heartache alone?
- ♥ Have I stopped and talked to my Heavenly Father about my hurts and trials? If not, what is holding me back?
- ♥ Am I only relying on family and friends to get me through my brokenness?
- ♥ Have I realized God can relate to many of my emotions and wants to go through it with me?

We often reach out to everyone except the One who can help us in times of need. I have prayed through so many times when my spirit was crushed, and sometimes it took years, but even during that time, I saw glimpses of prayers being answered and ways God was changing me through it. Allow God to comfort you in your brokenness, and trust Him to save you and your crushed spirit in His timing.

Father, sometimes I feel too broken to even say anything. Thank you for knowing my thoughts and understanding my hurts. I pray that you will comfort me and lift me up when I am too crushed to move. Thank you for being a God who understands. Help me through this, and help me trust in you for peace and strength. Amen.

Scroll Scriptures Before Social

"For everything that was written in the past was written to teach us, so that through the endurance taught in the Scriptures and the encouragement they provide we might have hope. May the God who gives endurance and encouragement give you the same attitude of mind toward each other that Christ Jesus had.
Romans 15:4-5

I was in the middle of a fascinating article on a rare disease that affected the life of a well-known celebrity when I realized I was supposed to be finding a recipe for a different way to cook the chicken sitting in my fridge. I only realized this because my husband called to tell me he was on his way home. I looked at the clock and saw it was 5:30 p.m. I started looking for the recipe around 4:15 p.m.! How did I get so sidetracked? Granted, I am the worst at finding a spoiler for a popular show when trying to find a how-to article on getting hard water stains out of a toilet!

Have any of you ever gotten distracted when searching for something? How many of you look things up online when you have a question? I look up everything from recipes and how-to articles to math problems to help my kids, diseases, illnesses, and shows, along with people who star in the shows. I'm sure none of you waste any time on social media, either. Ha!Ha! I'm probably the only one who finds herself mindlessly scrolling through the feed, wasting time but not really learning anything important.

What about when you have questions about parenting? What if you need direction or encouragement? Did you know God left the Bible and uttered every word so we would have a reference book to guide us and give us hope until he returns? He wants us to have answers, hope, and unity.

God has never been more clear with direction than when my husband and I were trying to decide where to move. We had outgrown the house we were in with the birth of our third child. We were looking at houses to buy, and we had a contract on one contingent on selling our home within a certain amount of time. Then, one day, my husband found this lot for sale and called me from work to ask me to go by and take a look at it. I told him it was crazy, but I drove by the lot, and I loved the location. It was the first time I had ever looked at a lot and could actually picture a house built on it. I told him logistically it couldn't work. We had a contract on a different house, and it would cost much more to build than to buy. He said, "Let's pray about it. If it's meant for us, then our house won't sell within the allotted timeframe, and we just won't renew the contract." So we did pray, and we enlisted the help of my mom, who is one of my strongest prayer warriors. In a few days, my mom called me, and she said, "Amy, I think I have an answer for you." I listened as she described going into her "prayer closet" and talking to God. She said she normally reads her devotion book first and then prays, but this time, she prayed first. This was her prayer, "Lord, you know Amy and Brad love you and want to honor you with what you have blessed them with. We know you can speak to us through prayer, songs, and scripture. We ask that you let them know the right decision to make that is in your will for them. In Jesus name, Amen." When she finished her prayer, she opened her devotion book to that day's devotion, and the scripture for it was from Haggai 1:7-8: "Go up to the hills and bring wood and build the house, that I may take pleasure in it and that I may be glorified, says the Lord." That story still gives me chills. This shows that God cares about the little things. He helps us with parenting, but he also cares when we have other issues causing us concern or when we need answers.

We as moms can have unity in the spirit when we look to Scripture for advice on parenting and encouragement and anything else we may need. The back of my Bible features a glossary of terms arranged alphabetically, covering everything from affliction and backsliding to blessings, criticism, decision-making, disobedience, rebellion, rejection, wisdom, and more. It's a great tool if you are looking for Scriptures on a certain subject. There are free Bible apps you can download to make it easier for you to read His word no matter where you are. Bible Gateway is one that offers a daily verse sent to your inbox, reading plans, an audio version, etc. Set a timer in the morning to intentionally spend time in His word. Start your day with God. God spoke His words and recorded them by prophets and His chosen followers so we could have a guide to help us navigate life. He wrote it to teach us. He wrote it so that we might have hope. 2 Timothy 3:16 tells us that all scripture is inspired by God and is valuable for teaching and providing guidance on how to live.

If you look up anything today, look up Scriptures on hope and encouragement. They are there. He left them for you. Share one with a friend who may need some encouragement. We could all use a little hope on any given day.

Moment to Reflect:

♥ How much time do I spend looking up information online?

♥ How much time do I spend scrolling through social media?

♥ Do I ever use my Bible as a reference for parenting questions?

♥ Do I have a friend or family member I can share an encouraging verse with today?

I am so guilty of wasting time on things that do not provide any positive benefit. I want to challenge you to spend more time in God's Word. When you have a question about any subject, start with the Bible and look up God's Word first before you explore other options.

Father, thank you for leaving me a road map to follow with verses that give hope and encouragement. I pray that I will take time to truly look at your Word when I have a situation and need guidance. Thank you for the unity it brings to believers when we come together in our faith and follow your Word. Help me to share hope with others who may need to hear it today. Amen.

Tank on Empty? Fill It Up!

"Therefore encourage one another and build each other up,
just as in fact you are doing."
1 Thessalonians 5:11

It was one of those days you wish you could redo. My girls were in elementary school, and my son was just three and still home with me. We had played that day, and I had tried to get him to take a nap so I could get a few things done. He didn't settle for his nap until a few minutes before I had to leave for the carline, so it took longer to wake him up, and I was running behind to pick up the girls. I went a different way and was going slightly over the speed limit when I was pulled over. Luckily, I only got a warning, but my three-year-old was amazingly awake to tell his sisters when they got in the car. We drove out of the school and onto the main road, and I was stopped at a red light when the mom behind me was not paying attention and ran into my back bumper. I got out and didn't see any damage. After a sob story from her about how her husband was going to be so mad, I told her it was fine, but I didn't get any info, and we parted ways.

We got home, and my kids couldn't wait to tell my husband about my day when he got home. "Mommy got pulled over by a policeman and got her car hit too!" With a roll of my eyes, I assured my husband it was just a warning, and I didn't see any damage to the back of my car. He went out to the garage to check it out. When he turned the car on and put it in reverse, the backup camera was damaged. We had to take it to get it fixed and replace the entire bumper, which was a $1,500 mistake on my part. I felt awful, and honestly, I felt like I couldn't do anything right. I was so upset that I went back to our room to let myself have a good cry. My door opened, and my sweet little boy crawled up onto my lap and said, "It's okay, mommy. You didn't mean to get hit, and you didn't get a ticket. I wuv you." He gave me a big hug, and just like that, my horrible, messed up, unproductive day turned a lot brighter.

When the day keeps piling on, it can be overwhelming, and your nerves feel as if one more thing could send you into a meltdown of catastrophic proportions. You feel down, discouraged, frustrated, maybe a little angry, and completely done. Then, just when you think you can't take one more thing, you get a text, a call, or someone gives you a great big hug, and suddenly, your day is better. You just needed that encouragement to build you up. The disciples felt like this in John 21 when they had been fishing all night long and caught nothing. Jesus came along and asked them if they had any food. When they told him no, he told them to throw their nets on the right side of the boat, and they would find some. They did just as he instructed, and their nets held so many fish they had trouble pulling them up. Sometimes, it just takes one small thing to make a huge difference!

Encouragement is huge. We all need it, and we can all give it to others. If someone comes to mind during the day, shoot them a quick text. Take time to call or text someone if you think of something positive to share with them. You may think it is little and wouldn't matter either way, but I promise you it does.

When our tank is empty, we all need to be filled with encouragement. Encouragement from other moms is great, too, because we are always comparing ourselves to other moms. It's nice when I have gotten a call or text from another mom who brags about one of my kids or tells me they love something specific I did. It means more coming from a fellow mom. I had a good friend call me after we lost our dog. She offered to drop everything she was doing and go walk with me or cry with me, whatever I needed. It encouraged me to know I had someone who cared when I was down. Hanging out with encouraging friends is a great way to lift yourself up. No one needs negativity, so distance yourself from others who only tear you down. Send them an encouraging text though. Even negative Nancy needs encouragement!

Moment to Reflect:

- Have you ever had your day changed from an encouraging text or call?
- Have you ever disregarded an urge to encourage someone because you thought it would not matter?
- Do you surround yourself with people who will lift you up?
- Have you prayed about lifting someone up who is negative or has been discouraging to you before?
- Pray for an opportunity to be an encourager and for God to give you the boldness to do so.

There is no doubt that a kind gesture, a reassuring smile, or an uplifting text could go a long way in making someone's day go from terrible to at least tolerable. Will you be obedient if you feel God urging you to reach out to someone to lift them up?

Father,

I have had days when a kind word has been all that has gotten me through. Will you help me to look for ways to encourage others and take opportunities to build someone up? I know you know what they are going through. Help me to be a light even when I do not know what is going on in their life. Amen.

Fizzled or Finished?

"For it is God who works in you to will and to act in order to fulfill His good purpose."
Philippians 2:13

D oes anyone else have any unfinished projects? You had the best of intentions. You planned everything out. You started out great but fizzled before you could finish. We have all been there. I have a craft room full of great ideas that never come to fruition. We still have the baby bed from when our three children were small. My husband began turning it into a bench but never finished the project. (Our youngest is 17 years old).

As a mom, I know God grows and changes us to help us become who we were meant to be. God has our best intentions in mind, and He has our path planned out. Sometimes, we are the ones who veer from the path. Luke 15: 11-32 is a great example of a son veering from the path his father had planned for him. The son made some bad choices, but eventually, he came back, and the father welcomed him with open arms. This is just like our Heavenly Father. No matter how many times we go against God's plan or our children turn down the wrong path, God welcomes us back and still wants to put us on the right path toward a great purpose.

25

Even when we take a turn or completely turn down a different road, He readjusts His course. From the day we accepted Him into our lives, He began a work in us. He has brought us through joys, trials, disappointments, triumphs, and defeats because He is continuing that work in us. As moms, we are put to the test with our children. When we are discouraged and don't know what to do, God will see us through. He is still working in us when we are scared, frustrated, or defeated in parenthood.

God might be at work in your life even if you don't realize it. During tough times, He offers comfort through prayer or wise advice from those who have been in your shoes. When you're feeling weak, He provides strength, sometimes through hope or unexpected opportunities that help you overcome challenges. If you're unsure about your purpose or direction, He can guide you by stirring your spirit or arranging circumstances that point you toward the right path.

God also supports your growth and transformation by helping you learn from your experiences. As you face difficulties, you develop empathy and compassion. At times, He provides the resources or support you need most. He offers physical healing and emotional restoration when you need it. When you seek wisdom, He provides clarity and insight into your situations. For encouragement, He connects you with supportive relationships and a sense of belonging.

Until Christ returns, God is carrying on his work. No matter how old our children get, our work is never quite over because they will always need us. Don't ever doubt that! The same is true for us as God's children. He works in us all the time and will continue to do so until His purpose is complete.

Isn't it good to know that we, as God's children, will always need Him, and He will always be working in us?

Moment to Reflect:

- ♥ Do you believe God has begun a good work in you and is working in your life?
- ♥ Are you confident that God will not leave you unfinished as He works in your life?
- ♥ Have you seen God work through trials and disappointments in your life? If so, what has God taught you about himself, and how could this help you when you face a new trial?
- ♥ Have you thanked God lately for never giving up on you and staying with you until the end?

What a comfort to know that He continues to work in our lives until we are complete. No matter what I do or how I veer from the path God has chosen for me, He continues to work in me until I am complete in Him.

Father,

I struggle in my own life sometimes with beginning things and not seeing them through. Thank you for telling us in Your Word that You will start a good work in us and carry it through to completion and for encouraging us to be confident in that promise. That gives me hope that you will never give up on me. I praise you for never leaving me unfinished. Amen.

Anxiety

"The very fact that you worry about being a good mom means that you are one."
—Jodi Picoult

Freedom From Fear

> "I sought the Lord, and He answered me; He delivered me
> from all my fears."
> Psalms 34:4

How many times a day do we worry? If you have an infant, you worry if your baby is developing as well as others. You worry if they are getting enough sleep or enough nutrition when they eat. You worry about germs or when they have a fever. As they start toddling around, you worry they will fall and hurt themselves or what they may stick in their mouth, nose, or ear. When they start school, you worry about how they will do in school and who their friends will be. The older they get, the more anxiety it seems to cause.

Preteens and teens take on an entirely different level of anxiety. They are beginning to want more independence and trying to figure out who they are and where they fit in. Peer pressure, grades, cell phones, social media, and dating all factor in as we moms try to be there for our kids. It is hard to teach them right and wrong and take a stand when you feel like you are the only mom doing so. I have literally had anxiety that has made me physically sick.

It is important to remember that when you get overwhelmed, you need to seek the Lord. No issue is too small for Him. You will hear me mention several times about being overwhelmed because it is a real problem. In another devotion, I mentioned when I had taken on too much with my kids' classrooms and PTO, etc. One beneficial suggestion from my husband was to spend my time doing the things that allow me to spend time with my kids and give up the positions and projects that are just busy work behind the scenes. Please hear me say that all positions are important, but if you are overwhelmed, you must make some hard choices about what to let go of. When deciding between roles that involved frequent non-child-related tasks like fundraising, event planning, and meetings unrelated to my child or classroom, it was straightforward for me to prioritize and let go of some of those commitments. Ask God to help you prioritize what matters most. He cares about your anxiety.

Some of you may be dealing with anxiety disorders that feel beyond your control. For those of us who haven't experienced this, it can be hard to fully grasp what you go through. After doing some research, I realized that the anxiety some of you face can be overwhelming compared to what I've experienced. People with anxiety disorders often have persistent, uncontrollable worry. They may experience intense fear and dread and sometimes panic attacks that lead them to avoid certain situations altogether.

Physically, anxiety can cause irritability, a racing heart, muscle tension, fatigue, sleep problems, digestive issues, and even sweating and trembling. Behaviorally and socially, it can lead to avoidance of situations or perfectionism due to a fear of making mistakes. Anxiety disorders can strain relationships, impact work or school performance, and diminish overall quality of life.

However, living with anxiety does not have to define or ruin your life. God is there to support those who struggle with these challenges and desires to help with your anxiety.

If you struggle with anxiety disorders, remember you are never alone. Christian counselor Liz Miller says, "Your frustration with the power that anxiety has in your life is shared by many Christians. Your anxiety is a shared struggle, not a shameful secret." God can offer peace and comfort to help manage distressing moments. Our faith can provide wisdom and direction, allowing us to take our thoughts captive, as described in 2 Corinthians 10:5: "We take captive every thought to make it obedient to Christ." This means we can choose to surrender anxious thoughts to God.

Being part of a faith-filled community can also be encouraging. God can work through mental health professionals who provide tools and therapies to help manage anxiety. Our faith offers a sense of purpose and a positive perspective on life. Grounded in our beliefs, we know we are unconditionally loved and accepted by God despite our struggles. Combining spiritual support with professional therapy can be a powerful way to manage anxiety.

Many times, our fears are warranted, but sometimes we may be afraid because we are relying on ourselves to handle a situation instead of asking for God's direction. He doesn't want us to worry. He tells us in Matthew 6: 25-33 we don't need to worry. When you worry, your mind pulls in many different directions. You don't always think rationally when you worry. In his book *Traveling Light,* Max Lucado talks about worry. "Worry divides the mind. The biblical word for worry (merimnao) is a compound of two Greek words, merizo ("to divide") and nous ("the mind"). Anxiety splits our energy between today's priorities and tomorrow's problems. Part of our mind is on the now; the rest is on the not yet. The result is half-minded living."

The Greek word translated as "anxiety" in the New Testament is "merimna" and it means being pulled apart and divided. This is exactly how our mind works when we worry. We focus on what could happen in the future instead of what is happening now. Give your worry to God. He will answer you when you seek Him. He can take all of your pieces that are divided and put them together to make you whole. Let Him deliver you from your fears.

Let these words from Liz Miller encourage you today, "However you come by your anxiety - trauma, heredity, for reasons unknown - you are not abnormal, disgraced, or unqualified to be who God called you to be."

Moment to Reflect:

♥ Do you make yourself sick worrying over your children?
♥ What specific things do you worry about when it comes to your children?
♥ How do you handle fears when you have a situation with your child that worries you?
♥ Have you asked God for help when you have anxiety over an issue? What does God say about your fear?
♥ Think of a time when you were concerned and turned to God for help. How did He calm your fears?

Being a mom is no joke. It is stressful, challenging, overwhelming, and can cause major anxiety if we let it. Pray, read your Bible, seek people who love Jesus, follow Him when you are struggling with worry, and let Him take away your fears.

Father,

You have given me the honor and privilege of being a mom. Some days are extremely rewarding, but some days can be challenging. When I have days when the anxiety is overwhelming and my worry makes me afraid, help me to seek you. Please calm my fears and help me to trust in you. Amen.

DAY NINE

Restlessness to Rescued

"The Lord hears his people when they call out to Him for help.
He rescues them from all their troubles."
Psalm 34:17 NLT

Your husband's company has been bought out, and you aren't sure if he will keep his job or be replaced. You had a routine doctor's appointment, and they discovered something abnormal and wanted to conduct further tests. One child has been struggling with a class at school, while another has had issues with a friend group. Can anyone relate? Everything may be fine one minute, and your entire world is turned upside down the next. It's hard not to dwell on what is happening and worry about the outcome.

When we sit and dwell on every possible scenario of what could happen in our situation, we are basically telling God we don't trust him to handle it. We will agonize over something to the point of making ourselves sick because we think of what could happen. Anxiety hinders us from living life with a faith that will get us through financial, health, and relational struggles.

As moms, we are not immune to struggles of every kind. We take the weight of the world on our shoulders as we try to protect our children and our families. When we let anxiety take over, we become distracted, and it keeps us from trusting in God to handle the situation. My husband is in the banking industry and worked for the same bank for 24 years until it was bought out. We had a valid reason to be anxious about the uncertainty of his job and the possibility of having to move to find work. We knew God had provided for us for many years, and He would continue to do so no matter what. We put the situation in His hands and asked for strength, provision, and the faith to trust Him no matter what. My husband was offered a position at a different bank, and we were able to stay in our town and not have to move. He loves his current job, and we saw God's hand at work in every aspect of the situation.

When we cry out to God, He hears us. When we are anxious about a situation, instead of dwelling on it and worrying until we are sick, we need to give our concerns to God and let him rescue us. He promises in His Word that He will be there to hear and be there to rescue. Don't struggle alone when you have a loving God ready to help you. He tells us in 1 Peter 5:7 to cast all of our anxieties on Him because he cares for us.

Don't go another day with worry and anxiety. Let Him take the weight away.

Moment to Reflect:

♥ Do you dwell on fears to the point of making yourself sick or distracting yourself from doing your daily responsibilities?

♥ Have you tried praying and asking God to take your fears and rescue you where you are struggling?

♥ How does knowing you *can* give Him your fears change your mindset?

♥ When your mind starts to worry, do you turn to Him or try to handle it on your own?

Praise Him in prayer and while listening to Christian songs. Show Him that you know He is in control and that you trust Him to handle your situation, no matter what it is. It is so easy to say that we will cast our cares on God but not actually do it. The first thing we tend to do when we get sad news or something bad happens is worry. We start imagining all the possibilities of what could happen until we make ourselves sick. We must consciously decide to give it to God and let it go. Daily. When we start to fear, we need to ask God to sustain us and strengthen our faith. He will never let us fall.

Father,

I am a worrier, and I will make myself sick without your help. Would you help me cast my cares on you when I am anxious? Please sustain me and hold me up when I struggle. Thank You that You made me righteous through You, and You promised in Your word never to let the righteous fall. I'm trusting in you to get me through. Amen.

Safe Haven

"Come to me, all you who are weary and burdened, and I will give you rest. Take my yoke upon you and learn from me, for I am gentle and humble in heart, and you will find rest for your souls."
Matthew 11:28-29

Have you ever been so tired or stressed as a mom that you just wanted to curl up and rest? Being a mom can drain you not only physically but emotionally as well. We pour ourselves into these precious lives Jesus has entrusted us with, and sometimes, it can be overwhelming. Jesus is asking us in our verse today to come to Him when we are weary and burdened. He wants to give us rest, a haven to come to when we are completely spent.

Not only does He want to give us rest, but He also wants us to take His yoke upon us. What does that mean? Well, a yoke is used in farming to join two animals together so they can share the workload. It makes the workload more even and productive. Many times, an older, more experienced animal is joined with a younger one to help train the younger one. The older one would be the designated leader, and the younger one would follow. They can't go in opposite directions. This is a great illustration of us with Christ. When we surrender to Him and let Him be in control, our burdens become light because we aren't trying so hard to fix something beyond our control. Jesus tells us in Matthew 11:30 that His yoke is easy, and His burden is light.

When Jesus says, "Take my yoke upon you and learn from me," He is saying He wants to help share our load and help train us so we can be more effective in life and the ministry of motherhood. We all have different ministries and purposes for which we were created. When we tackle our ministry and purpose with Jesus and allow Him to provide for our needs and take our stress and worries, it lightens our burdens. By combining my passion for creativity with teaching children's Sunday School and vacation Bible school, I enable Jesus to use my enthusiasm to demonstrate to kids, in relatable ways, the truth of the Bible and God's love for them. When I draw close to Jesus through prayer and devotion time, He helps me write devotions and inspirational blog posts that speak the message to people when they need to hear it. It's not me. It's me willing to let Jesus take that burden and make it light by coming along beside me and speaking truth to my mind, giving me the courage to write that truth for others to read. If we let Him take our burdens and learn from Him as He teaches us, He will share our load, and we will find the rest we seek.

In these verses, He mentions giving us rest and helping us find it on two separate occasions. I don't know about you, but when I have worries on my mind and feel overwhelmed, it's nice to have rest and share those struggles with someone who knows how to handle them.

Moment to Reflect:

- ♥ Do you need a place to find rest from being weary and having burdens that are weighing on you?
- ♥ Have you tried handling your burdens by yourself and just continue to feel overwhelmed and tired?
- ♥ What does God's invitation to rest for the weary and burdened tell you about who He is?
- ♥ Ask God to help you take His yoke and let Him share the load with you.
- ♥ Thank Him for providing the much-needed rest from all the worries of this world.

None of us can enjoy motherhood or our precious children when we are burdened by the extra weight of troubles, doubts, and fear. Jesus knows the value of taking on the weight of the world so we can have freedom. We don't have to do life alone. Take Jesus' yoke and let Him share the burden and the load so you won't be so overwhelmed. Find your safe haven in the one who wants to give you rest.

Father,

I have tried for too long to carry my burdens by myself. It's too much. I want to take your yoke so you can help me with my load. I pray I will find rest in you, and my ministry in motherhood will be more effective because my heart will become gentler and humbler like yours. Thank you for providing me with a safe haven to rest in. Amen.

When I am Weak, He is Strong

> "So do not fear, for I am with you; do not be dismayed, for I am your God. I will strengthen you and help you; I will uphold you with my righteous right hand."
> Isaiah 41:10

There are 365 times in the Bible that God says, "Do not fear," "Fear not," or "Do not be afraid." Wow! The God of the Universe knows I am prone to worry and need to be reminded daily not to fear. I literally have a verse for every day of the year that tells me not to fear.

God tells us not to fear because He doesn't want us to be preoccupied with anxiety and worry, missing out on all His blessings. When we are consumed with fear, we can't allow God to work in our lives and show us He has the power to change any situation we are worrying about. As a mom, when I let a situation with one of my kids consume me to the point of distress, I am so focused on the problem that I can't work with God to be part of the solution.

The second request He makes in our verse today is "Do not be dismayed." When you are dismayed, you are distressed.

Fear and distress go hand in hand. God is telling us that we shouldn't be distressed because he is our God. He's got this!

He promises in the next part of the verse to strengthen us and help us. He knows there will be times when we are weak. There will be times when we need to be held. He will be there to help us. If He is upholding us with His hand, He is right beside us, never far away. He is guiding us with his strength. Holding us with His right hand is important because the right hand symbolizes a place of honor, strength, and power in the Bible. God is telling us we do not have to worry. He has us! What a relief to realize that God knows what will happen, and He is telling us not to worry.

Moment to Reflect:

- ♥ If you struggle with fear, look up a different verse daily to help calm your fears. God provided you with 365 options to choose from.
- ♥ Knowing you are not supposed to fear means knowing you are also not supposed to be distressed. When you recognize you are distressed, hide this verse in your heart so you can fight off fear.
- ♥ Do you feel special and honored knowing God promised to uphold you with His righteous right hand?

Help fight your fear and anxiety by hiding Scripture in your heart that tells you not to be afraid. Ask God for strength and help when you are struggling with fear. I hope you feel cherished knowing that the God of the universe upholds you with his righteous right hand.

Father,

Sometimes, I let fear overtake me, and I forget that you are always with me. Help me not to get distressed when my life has problems. I pray I will rely on your strength to help me through whatever I face. Thank you for promising to uphold me with your right hand and making me feel honored and cherished. Amen.

Cripple My Fear with Control

> "When anxiety was great within me, your
> consolation brought me joy."
> Psalm 94:19

How can we experience joy amidst anxiety? Because God is in control and desires to alleviate our worries. Say Psalm 94:19, memorize it, pray it, and claim it so that anxiety will not take over and cripple you with fear. Throughout the entire chapter of Psalm 94, you see God is a just God. When we are tempted to think He doesn't see or hear or care what is happening with us, read this chapter and know that He does care, and although He disciplines us in love, He also seeks justice for those who are evil. When our peace is at risk, God not only offers us His word for guidance but also comforts us with His Spirit, enabling us to find joy instead of fear.

As moms, we cannot help but worry about our children, but worry can overwhelm us if we let it. We had a period when one of ours was having trouble with a friend group. Our child took a stand and was basically outed from the group of friends. As a mom, it is painful to see your child suffer, especially when they were doing the right thing and were excluded as a result. Social media makes it worse when you see posts of their friends hanging out without our child. When these situations happen, and they will, you must be strong as a mom and pray for God to give your child the strength and the faith to persevere even when it hurts.

Pray for friends who will be encouragers to your child and ones who will help them grow in their faith. Going through this situation taught our child empathy and helped form the characteristics she looked for in a friend. She is well-adjusted now with friends who lift her up, encourage her in her faith, and cheer her up when she has a bad day. As moms, we can't always stop bad things from happening, but we can teach our kids what to do when they occur. Be there to listen, but also help them to know what to look for in a friend and how to choose friends who will be encouragers and draw them closer to Christ. Always pray about it when you are anxious. God will give you the peace your momma heart needs so you can help your child with whatever situation they face.

You can literally make yourself sick with anxiety over all the things that could happen or go wrong... or you can give it to God. That peace is the best feeling in the world. It's knowing that everything may not be ok, but even if it's not, God is still in control.

Moment to Reflect:

♥ Are you making yourself sick worrying over circumstances that are out of your control?
♥ Have you hidden these eleven words from Psalm 94:19 in your heart so you can claim them when you are anxious and need joy?
♥ If something specific is causing you anxiety right now, surrender it to God and ask Him to replace your fear with peace.

The devil is out to destroy us and cripple us with fear and worry. We cannot let him win. When you feel that anxiety creeping in and the worry is overwhelming you, stop and ask God to take away your anxiety. His presence gives peace.

Father,

I refuse to let Satan destroy my life with fear and worry. I pray that no matter what is going on in my life, I will bring it to you and allow you to take that anxiety and fill me with peace. Give me the peace that passes all understanding and cripple my fear with the assurance that you are still in control, no matter what. Amen.

Enjoy the Day You Are In

"Therefore do not worry about tomorrow,
for tomorrow will worry about itself.
Each day has enough trouble of its own."
Matthew 6:34

Tomorrow has enough trouble, so just concentrate on today. Isn't that a relief? We can get caught up in looking at all that is happening to us, and we can overwhelm ourselves with worry. What this verse is saying is, don't borrow trouble. You don't know what is going to happen. If you look at this entire passage from Matthew 6: 25-33, you can see that God doesn't want us to worry about anything, including food, drink, or what we will wear. Even the birds don't have to store food in barns because He always provides for them. That may sound trivial, but if He cares about birds and making sure they are fed, how much more does He care about any problem we have? Matthew 6:26b says, "Are you not much more valuable than they?" The answer is Yes! You are much more valuable than the birds, and He cares about any troubles you have.

God is behind the scenes, orchestrating events that you do not even know about. The time you spend worrying about things that will happen tomorrow, you could be focusing on what is happening today and praying over that.

You can make yourself sick with worry for no reason. God knows all the troubles we are dealing with, and he doesn't want us to add more to our plate than we can handle. Tomorrow is an entirely different issue. If you stress and worry and focus on what could happen and all the things that could go wrong, you ruin the day you are in and could miss out on the joys God wants to provide.

Health scares are nerve-wracking, and as moms, we are not immune to getting the dreaded call from the doctor and worrying over what will happen to our kids if something happens to us. When my kids were in elementary school, I had a small skin tag that had to be removed near my collarbone. It was just a routine thing for my dermatologist to send a biopsy of it off to make sure it wasn't cancerous. When I got the call back from my doctor and heard a bunch of words before the word carcinoma, my life flashed before my eyes. I worried about my tomorrow and all my tomorrows. I thought about my kids and the time I wanted to spend with them.

I wish I had already committed Matthew 6:34 to memory when I went through this. I was able to have surgery to remove my skin cancer. I still need to have annual check-ups and must be very cautious in the sun, but I have come to realize that God has already planned for all my tomorrows. I want to live for today and enjoy every moment God has blessed me with. If I worry about what could happen, I miss out on all the joys God has in store for me today.

Hiding these verses in our hearts is essential because God can bring them to mind and help comfort us when a stressful moment arises or we are anxious about something. There is no need to spend hours stressing and worrying about what could happen when we can choose to focus on the good and have faith that God will be there for us no matter what happens.

Choose to have faith. Choose to believe that good things can happen. Choose to trust in the power of prayer. Do not worry about tomorrow. It steals your joy.

Moment to Reflect:

- ♥ Do you come up with all the scenarios that could happen and stress about it?
- ♥ Is your faith strong enough to overcome the anxiety you have so you won't worry about tomorrow?
- ♥ Can you commit this verse in Matthew to memory and ask God to help you not to worry when stressful situations arise?

Don't let Satan ruin your tomorrow. He wants you to live in fear. He wants you to worry. He wants to steal your joy. Trust in God for all outcomes, and enjoy the day you're in!

Father,

I choose not to worry about tomorrow. I know you hold the future, and my life is in your hands. Help me trust You to handle this situation and keep me from doubting Your power and love for me. I will have faith that You will provide hope for me regardless of the circumstances. Amen.

He Scouts Out the Safe Spots

"Be strong and courageous. Do not be afraid or terrified because of them, for the Lord your God goes with you; he will never leave you nor forsake you."
Deuteronomy 31:6

Can you imagine being part of a massive group of people who traveled together for over 40 years searching for a specific destination? What if you finally found that destination, but scary warriors lived there? This happened to the Israelites! Moses spoke what is recorded in Deuteronomy 31:6 to the Israelites before they were to take over the Promised Land they had been traveling towards for decades. If you read on to verses 7 and 8, Moses talks to Joshua and tells him that the Lord has gone on before them and will be with them.

Jesus goes before us regularly, just like God went before the Israelites into the Promised Land. He goes before us, scouts it out, and finds the traps and the treacherous places so he can come back and lead us down the safe path. He knows what is ahead, and that's why we can trust Him when He says not to be afraid. How often have we been terrified because we don't know the outcome? We don't know what is going to happen.

We must place our trust in the one who has gone before us to make a way.

Have any of you ever hired a guide to lead you somewhere you have never been? My husband and I went to a new destination for an anniversary trip, and we had several tours where we hired a guide to lead us. Our tour guides knew the terrain and the history with access to places outsiders do not. They took us to restaurants that offered local cuisines, and their knowledge of the area allowed us to see the land and hear its history through their eyes. They provided safety tips and saved us time because they knew the interesting places we would want to see. We didn't have to wander around aimlessly because they were ahead of us, leading us to the important sites. Jesus is our guide because He knows the way to navigate through this life. We must exercise faith to let Him lead us.

It is hard to step out and not know what is ahead, but Jesus is our light. He is the perfect choice for our guide because He has gone before us and knows the way. He directs us, leads us, and guides us. When we spend time in His word and learn the scriptures He gives us, we begin to hear and know His voice. The more we know His voice, the more we can differentiate it from this world. Psalm 119:105 says, "Your word is a lamp for my feet, a light on my path." Jesus truly is our light to guide our way.

Sometimes, we mess up, stumble, or take a wrong turn. Those are the times we don't follow our guide, going down a different path than the one He directed us to take.

When will we learn that He wants to be there for us? He wants to lead and guide us. We weren't meant to be afraid or terrified in this life. He is right here with us.

Moment to Reflect:

- ♥ Do you choose your path with or without a guide to help you?
- ♥ Do you have anxiety and discouragement about decisions you need to make or paths you need to take?
- ♥ There are three important things you can do to keep yourself from being afraid or discouraged:
  - Study God's Word and find Scripture passages about overcoming fear and anxiety. Memorize them!
  - Pray constantly and tell God your fears. Listen to His Spirit to calm you and give you the peace you need.
  - Praise Him as you worship Him. You can use a small Bluetooth speaker and connect it to your phone and play worship music as you work or throughout your home. When we are singing and worshiping, it takes our minds off fear and helps us realize who is in control.

If God stayed with the Israelites for 40 years and kept His commitment to lead them to the Promised Land, don't you think He will help you and guide you on the right path for your life?

Father,

I want to be strong and courageous. I need your help to guide me in the decisions I need to make in my life. Help me to trust you to direct me down the path I need to go. I know you will never leave me or forsake me because you keep your promises. Amen.

Strength

"The strength of a mother is unmatched. It's the kind of strength that emerges not from physical prowess but from the depth of love and responsibility she holds for her family. This profound sense of purpose drives mothers to accomplish what once seemed impossible."
–Elena Biedert

Stuck Like Glue

"Have I not commanded you? Be strong and courageous. Do not be afraid; do not be discouraged, for the Lord your God will be with you wherever you go."
Joshua 1:9

Have any of you ever tried to get certain glues off your fingers? Spray adhesive does not wash off very well, and dried hot glue lingers in weblike flutters. Don't even get me started on super glue. You need a file or sandpaper for that one. We do not have to be strong on our own. Today's devotion title is stuck like glue because we need faith that God will provide for us when we are weak. He is the strength that holds us together and stays with us when we are afraid.

How many times as a mom do we need someone to say to us, "Don't be afraid. Be strong"? How many times have we struggled to pull ourselves together when going through a difficult time with one of our children? I find it interesting that this verse is very similar to yesterday's verse but is in a completely different book of the Bible. Let me set the story for you. Joshua is the new leader of the Israelites after the death of Moses, and he needs to take possession of the land God promised them. The inhabitants of the land are giants, and Joshua will have to fight battles to finally claim this land they have sought for 40 years. The Lord is telling Joshua to be strong and courageous. He is telling him not to be discouraged or afraid. Why? Because God was telling Joshua that He would be with him wherever he went. God didn't say Joshua wouldn't have scary times. God doesn't say we won't have tough times. We may face some extremely intimidating times, but we don't have to be afraid or discouraged because God will be with us just like He was with Joshua.

That means so much to me as a mom, as a Christian, and as a person. For God to say multiple times, "Be strong and courageous. Do not be terrified or discouraged," means He truly wants us to know He will be there for us.

Have you ever had a situation where you needed to count on a friend or loved one, and they weren't there for you? I experienced a situation like this when my sister was sick with cancer. Some friends I believed I could depend on for support were surprisingly absent when I needed them. It hurts and can make you afraid to trust again. God provided new friendships throughout this time to encourage and lift me up when I least expected it. Friends who sent me devotions, prayers through text, Scriptures to encourage me, meals for my family, encouragement, and even gifts to my sister to comfort her! Our God won't leave us when we need Him most. We can trust His strength.

Jesus will be with us like super glue. He won't leave. You can't file or sand Him away. That gives me strength to make it through the day.

Moment to Reflect:

- ♥ Have you had a situation with yourself or your children when you were afraid or discouraged, and God provided strength through an unexpected source?
- ♥ Have you seen God work through another person to give you encouragement, or have you felt led to encourage someone else and knew it was God asking you to act on His behalf?
- ♥ Commit today's verse to memory to help you be strong when you face tough times.

God stuck with the Israelites and Joshua like glue. He was there for them even when they were stubborn, complained, griped, and disobeyed Him. It's harder to be afraid when you know Jesus is right there with you.

Father,

My strength must come from you. I don't have enough on my own. Help me commit this verse to memory so that when I face trials, I will remember not to be anxious or afraid but to trust that you will be there to guide me. Amen.

DAY 16

Stand Firm

"Be on your guard; stand firm in the faith;
be courageous; be strong.
Do everything in love."
1 Corinthians 16:13-14

Why would we, as moms, need to be on our guard? I can think of a list of reasons:

- Satan wants to destroy families.
- Social media and other influences can impact our kids in a negative way.
- Our children's friends are not all being raised with the same values as our children.
- Public schools are incorporating more anti-Christian views into the classroom.
- Temptation to compare ourselves and where we are with others' journeys and make assumptions that others don't go through what we do.

These are just a few of the many reasons we need to remain on guard.

You are helping yourself to stand firm in the faith now by setting aside time for God, committing scripture to memory, praying, etc. Also, don't allow your child to participate if you know something is wrong. Stand firm. So many parents these days give in because they want their children to like them. It's not an issue of them liking us. Chances are, if you stand firm in your faith, they may not like you because it goes against what society deems appropriate. Galatians 1:10 says, "Am I now trying to win the approval of human beings, or of God? Or am I trying to please people? If I were still trying to please people, I would not be a servant of Christ. This verse is telling us to stand firm in what we believe and do everything in honor of Christ, not what your child wants or what other moms are doing.

Be women of courage. It takes guts to stand up for what you believe in. It is not easy. It helps if you have another mom or two who can encourage you in your faith and help you be strong. Stick together! I have other moms in my life who share the same values; if I am questioning something, I will call them and see what they would do. I also meet with some moms regularly, and if anything needs to be discussed or I need their opinion, I will ask. I still pray about every decision, but sometimes it helps to have fellow moms standing in the gap.

Last but certainly not least, the end of our verse in Corinthians says, "Do everything in love." This is a hard one. Sometimes we want to lash out. Maybe we feel like the other person had it coming, or maybe our child went against everything we said, and they messed up. It doesn't matter if we feel someone deserves it or not; we still need to do everything in love. Whether it's your child making a poor decision or someone wronging you, and you respond with love, you are creating an opportunity for Christ to step in and transform a heart and a life.

Moment to Reflect:

- ♥ Am I standing guard over my children to protect them from outside influences that can lead them astray?
- ♥ What am I doing to stand firm in my faith? Is my relationship with Christ where it needs to be so I can keep my faith strong?
- ♥ Have I befriended other moms with the same values and beliefs who can help me have the courage to stand up for what is right?
- ♥ Do I handle every situation with love?

These two verses pack a lot of punch! They give us several things to think about in only a few words. As a mom, I need to be on guard and be vigilant to know what is going on around me and in my home so I can keep Satan out of our lives. My faith needs to be strong, and my courage needs to be inspired by other like-minded moms so I have the strength to stand firm every day. I need to strive to handle every situation out of love so that others see Christ in me.

Father,

Help me to be on my guard to protect my children and my family from Satan. I pray I will stand firm and not sway in my commitment to keep negative outside influences and social media negativity away from my children. Give me the courage and strength to stand up for what I believe in and encourage other moms to do the same. Help me to love with the love of Christ in every situation. Amen.

Fly Like an Eagle

"But those who hope in the Lord will renew their strength. They will soar on wings like eagles; they will run and not grow weary, they will walk and not be faint."
Isaiah 40:31

Have you ever had a day when you just felt zapped? You literally felt like you had no energy at all. You're a mom, so of course, the answer is yes! We all have days when we feel tested, overwhelmed, weary, and completely drained.

Do you feel defeated? Do you feel like you try to be a good Christian mom, but all around you is corruption? Parents are letting their children do whatever they want? It may make you feel like a bad parent, even when you try to do the right thing.

We need to hope in the Lord when we feel there is nothing else we can do—when we feel like this world has turned its back on God and all things right. When our kids tell us they are the only ones who aren't allowed to go to a certain place, have a certain item, or dress a certain way, we still have hope. We remind ourselves that Christ is our hope.

I don't know about you, but I would love to soar on wings like eagles and run without growing weary. My husband and I have felt the sheer exhaustion that comes from not giving in. We have been the parents that wouldn't let our kids go to certain parties. We have been the parents who chose not to allow our children to spend the night at certain houses. We asked the questions, we checked the phones, we enforced the curfew, we took the keys, we confiscated the phone, and we grounded.

We also opened our home to their friends, allowed trust to be earned back, hosted sleepovers, after-dance parties, and church functions, and made exceptions to curfews when they stayed in touch or had special circumstances. Our strength came from the Lord when we were mentally and physically exhausted. We always had hope in every circumstance.

Are you experiencing difficult circumstances and wondering if there is any hope? Don't ever doubt it. Don't ever be so weary that you lose sight of your purpose. Don't ever feel bad for doing the right thing. Don't ever quit getting your strength from the Lord. He is there to lift us up. Go soar!

Moment to Reflect:

- ♥ When you feel completely drained, how do you get your strength to go on?
- ♥ Do you feel like you are one of the only parents who does the right thing anymore?
- ♥ When you feel defeated and overwhelmed, do you have fellow believers to offer you encouragement?
- ♥ Knowing that God never grows weary and that He renews our strength, does this alter your perspective on feeling weary?
- ♥ Commit this verse to memory for times when you feel weary and defeated!

This verse gives me hope that when I am completely overwhelmed by life, kids, and everything this world throws at me, Christ will take that weariness and replace it with strength that can only come from Him.

Father,

There are days when I am completely drained and feel like I have nothing left to give. I need your strength to pick me up and help me soar like an eagle. I place my hope in you and have faith that I won't grow weary. Amen.

Strength in the Savior

"I can do everything through Christ who gives me strength."
Philippians 4:13 NLT

As a Christian mom in the world today, do you ever feel a little like a small weakling with no armor up against a giant armed with every shield and sword imaginable? I definitely do! David did, too, but he conquered Goliath. Are you up against a wall, and you feel like you have nowhere to turn, and everyone is trying to pull you back and sway you to their side? Moses felt the same way running from the Egyptians before he parted the Red Sea and escaped. Have you ever been ridiculed as a mom for your faith or your stance on certain issues? Paul was beaten, stoned, shipwrecked, and thrown in jail for his faith, but he never gave in. These ordinary individuals, who became heroes of the faith, accomplished this through the strength provided by Christ. We, as moms, have that same ability to accomplish great things through the strength we get from Christ.

Fighting giants, parting seas, and being sent to jail are all circumstances that could use some supernatural strength. In each one of these situations, God was in control and showed His strength and power to overcome their challenges. I may not have had to fight a giant Goliath or run from an army, but sometimes, I feel like I need extra strength to handle a situation. Raising Christian kids in a world that bombards them with ads and posts and influencers who want them to think and act and do what the world does is difficult. I feel like I am fighting against the current, and it takes every bit of strength I have to just stay afloat. I want to be a mom who raises the next generation to love Jesus, to put Him first, to keep their values and morals, to stand firm in their beliefs, regardless of what others do. It's tough being a Christian mom. I have to keep my focus on what matters. God has sent me strength many times in the form of another mom standing with me on an issue that others disagreed on or another mom giving me an encouraging word. I know the uplifting words came from God, but they were being obedient to listen to God and deliver them.

Paul wrote the book of Philippians in the Bible for the Christian church he established in Philippi. Today's verse from Philippians was written to encourage those reading it that they can survive whatever life throws at them through God's strength. Paul was so focused on the strength that came from Christ that he considered his imprisonment as an opportunity to further his ministry in Rome. He was whipped and beaten in prison, but he prayed and sang hymns. He was isolated and lonely but wrote encouraging letters to the churches because he wanted them to grow. He had friends who betrayed him. He had many sleepless nights. He had every reason to be bitter and just give up, but he didn't. He relied on the strength of the Savior.

You may be fighting your own giants or parting your own seas. You may have to pray for tough love for a child who has gone astray. Siblings or a spouse or friend may have betrayed you. You may have made some bad decisions and now face consequences that scare you. Whatever the situation you find yourself in, know that God will give you the strength to get through it. Commit this verse to memory so that when you are in a tough situation, you can say this in your heart, and God will hear it and give you the strength you need to overcome anything.

Moment to Reflect:

- Are you fighting any giants today? (It could be a boss, a co-worker, someone you thought was a friend, etc.)
- Are you struggling in a situation with your child and don't feel like you have the strength to do what needs to be done?
- Do you allow God to be part of your decisions and your dilemmas, or do you try to handle problems on your own?
- What changes can you make to center your decisions around Him instead of handling them on your own?
- Commit this verse to memory for times when you face obstacles and situations that require more strength than you have!

Looking at all the people who have gone before me and all they have endured through God's strength gives me hope. When I think about Goliath and a small boy with a slingshot, an entire sea parting to make room for millions to cross, or a man who sang praise songs in prison, I know there is a God who has the strength to help me with my problems.

Father,

No matter what I am going through, I know you are there and can help me through anything. Thank you for giving me the strength to make it when I feel like I am overwhelmed. Continue to encourage me and help me to hide this verse in my heart to give me strength when I am weak and discouraged. Amen.

Suit Up with Your Shield

"The Lord is my strength and shield. I trust him with all my heart. He helps me, and my heart is filled with joy. I burst out in songs of thanksgiving."
Psalms 28:7 NLT

We know the Lord is our strength, and we rely on that strength to get through hard times. The three words "and my shield" are extremely important in Psalm 28:7. What do you think of when you hear the word "shield"? I think of Captain America, knights in medieval times, and swat teams preparing to swarm into a hostile situation to provide protection and safety. A shield helps defend us from danger.

God not only provides us with strength but also serves as our shield, protector, safety, and security. He literally covers us and protects us from attacks from the enemy. When our hearts trust in Him, He helps us. He provides us with a shield of protection so the enemy can't defeat us.

Being a mom is a tough job. We don't receive very much appreciation, and sometimes, it feels like Satan is attacking you, your kids are against you, and even some other moms are not in your court! You need more than the Lord's strength. You need His shield of protection from the outside world!

What do you think of now when you hear the word "shield"? I picture a force field around me that protects me from Satan. I'm like a tortoise who crawls into his shell, protected from harsh elements and danger. We don't just have a shield. We have an entire arsenal of armor from God that can protect us from Satan. Ephesians 6:10-18 talks about the full armor of God. Our battle with the devil isn't against flesh and blood. We are up against principalities, powers, darkness, and wickedness. You need special armor for that! God's armor has a breastplate of righteousness that protects our hearts, footgear that allows you to tell others about the peace that comes from God, a helmet of salvation that protects our minds from doubting God, the Sword of the Spirit which is God's word (the Bible), and the shield of faith to protect us from Satan's insults, setbacks and temptations. No matter what Satan tries to defeat me with, he cannot get through the barrier and covering of Christ around me! It's time for you to suit up!

Moment to Reflect:

- ♥ Do you need more than just the strength Christ provides?
- ♥ Did you realize that you could have a shield of faith around you, protecting you from the enemy's attacks when you let your heart trust in God?
- ♥ Will you allow your heart to trust in God so He can help you?

Sometimes, I need more than strength in my life. I need God's protection as I struggle with attacks from all sides of the enemy. I need to let my heart trust in God, so He will help me through my struggles.

Father,

I don't have to be afraid of the enemy when I trust in you. No matter how many times he comes at me and how many ways he tries to defeat me, my strength to endure comes from you. Be my shield and my protector as I fight daily to do what's right as a mom and as a Christian. Amen.

He is My Hiding Place

"God is our refuge and strength, an ever-present help in trouble. Therefore we will not fear, though the earth give way and the mountains fall into the heart of the sea."
Psalms 46:1-2

Who do you run to when you are in trouble? Do you have a place where you seek refuge that makes you feel safe? Psalms 46:1 says God is our refuge. He is our safe place. He is our haven that we should run to when we are afraid or in danger.

Sometimes, we just need someone to tell us, "It's going to be okay" –that reassurance that the crumbling pieces of your life can be put back together. You need to know that even when everything around you falls apart, you have a refuge to run to. There have been times in my life that I don't think I would have made it through without seeking refuge in Jesus. I have experienced miscarriage and the death of a sibling. When your world is turned upside down, you need a hiding place. God gave me Scriptures during these sad times that comforted me. I know that God's Word is alive, and I know that it is God-breathed. When you read Scripture, it's not just old words on a page. It is as if God is in the room speaking the words directly to you, letting you know it's going to be okay! After my miscarriage and many years later when my sister passed away, we prayed for God to hold us and give us peace. We claimed the verses in Psalms 34: 17-18, which states, "The righteous cry out and the Lord hears them; He delivers them from all their troubles. The Lord is close to the brokenhearted and saves those who are crushed in spirit." We knew God heard us cry out, and He comforted us in our grief.

We got pregnant again after our miscarriage, but it was a rocky pregnancy. I had to go in weekly for 12 weeks for tests and then wait a couple of days each week for the labs to come back to see if my baby was okay. Those days each week were the longest two days ever, and I clung to Psalms 112:7: "He will have no fear of bad news; his heart is steadfast trusting in the Lord." My husband and I clung to that verse, and we prayed for God to protect our baby and keep it safe. God answered those prayers and gave us a beautiful baby girl.

We don't have to be afraid when it seems like our world is falling apart. We don't have to be scared or fearful when the storms of life come. We have a shelter. Sometimes, in the middle of a crazy day, we need to just shut the world out and connect with God in order to stay grounded. There are several things we can do to feel closer to God. Here are some examples:

Daily Practices:

- **Morning Quiet Time**: Start your day with a brief period dedicated to prayer, scripture reading, or a devotional. Use this time to center your heart and mind on God.
- **Intentional Moments**: Throughout your day, take moments to pause, take a deep breath, and either thank God for specific blessings or say a short prayer for someone else.
- **Gratitude List**: If you're feeling stressed, make a list of things you're grateful for. This practice can help shift

your focus from your troubles to the blessings in your life.

- **Scripture Reminders**: Write down scripture verses or inspirational quotes on index cards or post-it notes, and place them where you'll see them often to provide constant reminders of your faith.

Personal Retreats:

- **Create a Sanctuary**: Designate a special space in your home—a chair, loveseat, or small corner—with a few faith-based books. Use this area as your personal retreat for quiet reflection and relaxation.
- **Nature Walks**: Take walks outside to clear your mind and connect with God. Being in nature can offer a sense of peace and draw you closer to your spiritual life.

Engaging Practices:

- **Journaling**: Keep a journal to record your thoughts, reflections, and specific prayers. This practice helps you track your spiritual journey and keep focused on your spiritual goals.
- **Inspirational Music**: Listen to Christian or inspirational music while working, doing chores, or commuting. Let the music uplift your spirit and soothe your mind.
- **Pray Anytime, Anywhere**: Develop the habit of praying throughout your day. You can pray silently in any situation. If someone comes to mind, pray for them or express gratitude to God for the important people in your life.

Acts of Faith:

- **Helping Others**: Find ways to perform acts of kindness, even with a busy schedule. Helping others reflects your faith and can strengthen your sense of connection with God.

- **Reading Devotionals**: Incorporate reading devotional books into your routine, whether during your morning quiet time or lunch break. This helps you focus on spiritual matters despite daily distractions.
- **Group Worship and Bible Study**: Join a Bible study group or participate in group worship. Being part of a faith community provides spiritual support and opportunities for growth.

Moment to Reflect:

- ♥ When you feel down and discouraged, where does your strength come from?
- ♥ Do you consider Christ your refuge when your world is falling apart?
- ♥ Who do you turn to when you are in trouble?
- ♥ Knowing He created the mountains and the seas, it's comforting to know God is our refuge when the earthquakes of life come and rattle our very foundation.

I automatically turn to worry when I am going through trouble in my life. I need to remember that Christ is my hiding place when I am scared or need refuge. He can be my strength when I am weak.

Father,

In you, I have shelter in the storms of life. You never promised us that we would have it easy and everything would be perfect. You have promised that when the bad times come, and they will, you will be there to shelter us and keep us safe. Thank you for being there when my foundation is rattled to the core. It's comforting to have a refuge to run to. Amen.

Our Struggles Bring His Strength

"He gives strength to the weary and increases the power of the weak."
Isaiah 40:29

After enduring a miscarriage and several health-related issues, our doctor led my husband and me to believe if we were going to have children, we were going to need medical intervention. We prayed about the right thing to do, knowing it was completely out of our hands. We decided that we felt God telling us to trust in Him, not the doctors. The doctors were telling us to do one thing, but we decided to be faithful to what God was telling us. The next pregnancy was a rollercoaster ride, but she made it, and God got the glory! Three beautiful children later, we are living proof that when we are weak, God is strong.

Life is tough. Sometimes, you are faced with a choice, like we were, to trust God in the unknown. Sometimes, you must endure unimaginable hardships to make you stronger and force you to rely on God. I have found in my life that the times when I am struggling and having the most difficulties are the times I feel closest to God. Why is that? I think it's because when everything is going well, we don't call on Him. We believe we can handle things on our own. When the hard times come, and we don't know what to do, we rely on Him as our strength.

The next time you are struggling with something, be thankful even in your weakness. It sounds crazy, but your faith will grow stronger in hard times when you allow yourself to fully rely on God's strength to carry you through. James 1:3 promises this, "For you know that when your faith is tested, your endurance has a chance to grow." Sometimes, the hard times give us the ability to withstand more. It strengthens us.

Moment to Reflect:

- ♥ Think back to hardships and trouble in your life. How was your faith during that time?
- ♥ What are some ways you have experienced God's faithfulness during tough times?
- ♥ When you are facing trials and difficulties, do you delight in your weakness, knowing God will be strong for you?
- ♥ Does this verse give you hope to be able to handle persecutions and difficulties when they come your way?

We all want to curl up in a ball and hide under a blanket when our lives take a turn for the worse. Trials are complicated, and the struggles are real. When you start to feel weary because of your circumstances, ask God to send you strength. He may use a neighbor, friend, coworker, or your spouse, but He will send you strength when you need it most. Be looking for it and expect it!

God rewards our faith when our circumstances seem impossible. It's not easy to put all your trust in Him when reality steps in and fills you with doubt. Faith has to take precedence. Tell God that you trust Him, even when it doesn't make sense. When you do this, you will see your faith grow like never before!

Father,

There are times when I feel discouraged and don't understand why I am going through certain trials. When I am having difficulties, could you strengthen me as only you can and help me through the hardships, knowing that my weakness is where your strength flourishes? Amen.

Direction

"As your mother, I promise you that I will always be in one of three places: in front of you to cheer you on, behind you to have your back, or next to you so that you aren't alone."
—Helen Barry

Which Way Do I Go?

"A man's heart plans his way, but the Lord directs his steps."
Proverbs 16:9 NKJV

This verse should comfort those of us who are not sure if we are making the right decision. We have the Bible to guide us, Christian friends who can influence us, and the Holy Spirit living inside of us. Yet, we still try to do things *our* way. Knowing God is in control should give us peace, but so often, we stay conflicted and try to stay in the driver's seat.

We think we know what is best for our lives. Sometimes, we think we know what is best for our friends, loved ones, and our children, too. Ultimately, God has the final word in what happens, despite what we do. We can make plans, have goals, and map out exactly what we want to happen until the Lord comes along and directs our steps, sometimes in the opposite direction.

Isn't it ironic how we often pray for direction, only to be uncertain about following the path God leads us on? Even when we can't see what lies ahead, God does. His guidance is always the best because He can foresee obstacles and detours that we are unaware of. He is the most reliable map we can have.

God directed me in my dating life, steering me onto the path to meet my husband. I'm thankful for being obedient in where I went to college and where he led me to work for a summer job because each decision led me to meet my husband. Originally, I planned to become a defense attorney. I was passionate about the law and excited by the prospect of trying cases and uncovering evidence to clear my clients. I took Latin in high school because I researched and knew understanding Latin terminology would help me in researching all of the Latin-based legal terms. Yet, if I had chosen my way, I would never have been happy. I ended up with a Business Degree and chose to stay home when I had kids. The Lord directed my steps and knew what was best for me. He knew my heart.

Let this verse in Proverbs lead you as you let the Lord lead you and guide your steps.

Moment to Reflect:

- ♥ Do you leave God out when you make your plans?
- ♥ Have your plans ever been completely changed from what you originally set out to do or accomplish?
- ♥ If your plans have been changed before through God's intervention, which way was best?
- ♥ Have you been around the bend and realized why God directed things to happen the way they did?

Even though I love to make lists and always have my own agenda, I strive to ask God for direction when I have decisions to make. It saves me time in the end since He is going to accomplish His will regardless!

Father,

I have so many plans and goals I want to accomplish. I know you have plans for my life, too, and I want to be in your will as I make my decisions. Please guide me and direct my steps so I don't take a wrong turn on the path you already have laid out for me. Amen.

Trust in Him, Even If....

"Trust in the Lord with all your heart, and lean not on your own understanding; in all your ways submit to him, and he will make your paths straight."
Proverbs 3:5-6

I struggle with making decisions. I frequently seek advice when unsure what to do, but I don't always pray about it like I should. I need to acknowledge God in all things, even when they don't happen as planned.

How many times a day as a mom do you need direction? I need it all the time. Parenting is not for wimps! So often, I am in uncharted territory and have no idea what I'm supposed to do. This verse in Proverbs makes it seem so simple. I need to trust in the Lord with all my heart, relying on Him fully for every decision I make, no matter how minor. He cares about even the small details that we might think don't matter—because to Him, they do.

I do not need to lean on my own understanding. Ouch! How many of us try to make things work only if we can understand everything? Guess what? God's ways are not our ways, and sometimes, we do not (or won't) understand why He does things the way He does.

He just wants us to acknowledge Him. He wants us to give Him glory, even if we do not understand what is happening and cannot see Him at work. Even when it doesn't make any sense to us, He will give us direction. He will guide us toward the path we are supposed to take.

Moment to Reflect:

- ♥ Are you ever unsure of what to do when you have a big decision?
- ♥ When you have to make a decision, do you pray about it and ask for God's guidance, or just do what you think is right?
- ♥ Do you acknowledge God and give Him glory, even when what you are going through doesn't make sense?
- ♥ Have you had a situation where God led you in the opposite direction than the one you were going, but it turned out to be for the best?

As you think about this verse and these questions, I encourage you to think about the God we serve. We may face challenging situations with our kids, but He will walk through them with us. He doesn't leave us to face trials alone. Get to know Him more by reading the Bible, singing praise songs, worshiping Him, and praying. Choose to obey Him even when you don't understand, which will help you trust Him more and grow your faith. You can't grow in your Christian Walk if you don't face obstacles and challenges. Most importantly, learn to trust Him completely, leaving no room for any other option but Him!

Father,

I struggle with asking for help when I need it. I know you have a plan for my life, and you want what is best for me. I pray that when I have decisions to make, I will seek you and your guidance so that I won't waste time taking paths that were never meant for me to travel. Amen.

DAY 24

Real or Artificial?

"The Lord will guide you always; he will satisfy your needs in a sun-scorched land and will strengthen your frame. You will be like a well-watered garden, like a spring whose waters never fail."
Isaiah 58:11

I'm going to just come clean and admit that I don't have a green thumb. My kids make fun of me and ask me why I even buy real plants. They told me I would save money by just getting the artificial ones that won't die. Do you know why most of the plants I buy die? It's because I get busy, and I forget to water them! They wait out in sun-scorching weather for any hydration at all until they wither up and become brittle and brown. We have a garden in our backyard, and the only reason we can grow any food at all is because my husband had sprinklers installed so we could water the garden on a timer. The garden is different from my plants on other parts of our patio because the source of nourishment is different.

The people in Isaiah 58 weren't getting nourished from fasting and other religious routines. They were going through the motions, but they weren't truly helping people. If you study the entire chapter of Isaiah 58, the Lord is calling out the people with hearts that are not in tune with Him. He didn't want them to merely go through religious routines but to have hearts that showed mercy and love. If we fast and pray and just go through the motions, but our lifestyle and heart don't align with God, we have missed the point. The promise that the Lord will guide me means I don't have to wait for a timer to come on to remind Him that I need "watered" with His guidance. He cares for and is there for me because he loves me, satisfying my needs in a sun-scorched land and strengthening my frame. He doesn't leave me wandering in a lost world without direction or provision. He provides for my needs, whatever they are. When we are in tune with God and our hearts align with His, He provides continuous spiritual nourishment to us, which allows us to thrive like a well-watered garden.

As we grow closer to Christ and allow Him to give us that spiritual nourishment, our actions will be in tune with what God would want us to do. We will follow the nudges we get from His Holy Spirit to help those in need and have a heart for those less fortunate. Our children will learn so much just from our actions. They can tell the difference when you are going through the motions and when you genuinely care about something and want to make a difference.

Just as we need to water plants to keep them healthy, we must also care for ourselves physically, mentally, and spiritually. When we nurture our spiritual well-being, our relationships with our spouse and children tend to flourish, compared to when we are experiencing a "spiritual drought." The closer we grow to God, the more our hearts align with His, allowing us to offer more love to others.

I want my spiritual life to be like the well-watered garden. I want Jesus continually pouring into me and strengthening my faith so my heart breaks for what breaks His. I would love for all my plants to be well-watered, like the garden mentioned in Isaiah 58:11. I'm sure my plants would, too!

Moment to Reflect:

- ♥ Do you ever feel like my dry, thirsty plants, needing water and nourishment to grow?
- ♥ Do you wander around on your own, thirsting and struggling when you could be nourished by God daily?
- ♥ What can you do to nourish your soul and allow it to thrive?
- ♥ Trust in the one who promises to take care of your needs and strengthen you where you struggle.

I don't want to wander around struggling and withering away when I could be flourishing with God's help. I want Him to guide me, lead me, and nurture me into who I am supposed to be.

Father,

You know I do not always know the right direction to take. Thank you for promising to guide me and satisfy my needs when I am struggling. You nourish me and keep me flourishing instead of withering. I am grateful for your water that never fails. Amen.

Counseled By the Creator

*"I will instruct you and teach you in the way you should go;
I will counsel you with my loving eye on you."*
Psalm 32:8

I am the worst at trying to figure something out with only a set of directions. I can describe it all day long, but I like pictures, diagrams, and even, dare I say, a practice run if it's somewhere I am supposed to be. Psalm 32:8 says that God gets me. He knows I need more than just instructions. I need someone to teach me the way I should go.

When someone teaches you, they make sure you know the right thing to do so you don't feel lost. When someone teaches you, they use their knowledge and wisdom to help you understand something. When someone teaches you, they keep instructing you and guiding you until you learn.

Not only does God promise to teach and instruct me, but He also promises to counsel me. What does a counselor do? More than anything, I believe they listen and guide you in the way that is best for you.

Once God has instructed, taught, and counseled me, He still watches over me to ensure that I grasp the right direction and remain on the right path. These acts of guidance, teaching, and oversight truly reflect the care of a loving parent. Isn't that what we do for our children? We try our best to guide them with instructions and teach them the right way so they will make good choices. We listen to them when they need to talk and always watch over them, no matter how old they get, because we love them, and they will always be our children.

As a mother, wife, sister, daughter, friend, and Christian, I need all the guidance, teaching, counseling, and support I can get. Juggling these roles can be overwhelming, and it is incredibly comforting to know that as a child of God, I am not alone in this journey. He not only provides the instruction and wisdom I need but also offers ongoing counsel and watchful care. What a comfort to know I am a child of God, and He is willing to do all of that just for me and for you!

Moment to Reflect:

- ♥ Do you ever feel like some people instruct you but leave you hanging as far as what to do?
- ♥ Have you had a teacher who keeps pursuing different ways to teach you until the light finally goes off and you understand?
- ♥ Have you just sat and talked to God, shared your heart, and allowed Him to listen and counsel you in areas you need direction?

What an awesome God who stays to watch over us even as He teaches and directs us. He wants to make sure we are on the right path. I need all the help I can get when it comes to direction. I am the one who requires pictures to fully comprehend instructions and directions. I am so thankful God is a God who understands my struggles and meets me where I'm at. I'm grateful he is there to watch over me and counsel me when I need it.

Father,

How can I ever veer off on the wrong path when I have you to guide me every step of the way? Thank you for teaching in ways I can understand. Thank you for the wisdom you share and your wise counsel who listens and provides instruction to me daily. Continue to watch over me so that I won't take a wrong turn. Amen.

Be My Navigator in Life

"Show me your ways, Lord, teach me your paths. Guide me in your truth and teach me, for you are God my Savior, and my hope is in you all day long."
Psalm 25:4-5

Sometimes in life, we feel like we are going on autopilot without direction. We may be going through personal struggles in relationships. Our kids may be having a hard time, and we, as the parents, feel that struggle too. We may be dealing with a health crisis that is so overwhelming we feel like we are going in circles with no way out. What do we do when we pray and want to choose the right path but have no idea what that path is? We pray this verse. We seek God's wisdom. He is like a Waze map. If any of you have this app on your phone, you know it is a great way to put in the address you want to go to and figure out the best route to get there. It allows other Waze users to report when there is a wreck up ahead that could delay you, a hazard or pothole in the road, or a car stalled on the roadside, and my personal favorite is when it informs you of police cars ahead. God also knows what is ahead on our path. He knows the obstacles we can't see. He knows all the different paths to get us to the same place without the roadblocks.

"Show me your ways, O Lord, teach me your paths." When we pray and ask God to show us His ways and paths, we are telling Him that we want to be in alignment with His will is for our lives. We are telling Him that we don't want to waste time going on our own path, which sometimes leads us away from where we need to be. We want to be on the path He has already chosen for our lives.

When we ask for direction in a situation, and He gives us an answer, we need to follow His way even if it doesn't make sense. Sometimes, He can see what is around the bend when all we see are clear roads.

When we ask for guidance in His truth and for Him to teach us, we are including Him and acknowledging that He knows the way. We are showing Him that we know He can instruct us when we don't know the answers.

Acknowledging Him as our God and Savior and putting our hope in Him is the ultimate reflection of our trust in Him and shows we have faith that He will get us through the situation.

Moment to Reflect:

- ♥ What is your first reaction when faced with a trial?
- ♥ Do you panic and get stressed when you have a crisis, or do you turn to God?
- ♥ If you don't like the direction God is sending you, do you go your own path?
- ♥ How strong is your faith? Are you able to completely place your trust in God to handle your situation when it seems impossible?

Oh, how I need to commit this verse to memory for myself. How many times have I taken the wrong path because I didn't bother to ask God for directions? God is truth, and He is light, and He wants the very best for us in all situations. He knows what is up ahead, around the corner, over the mountain, and beyond the bend. Trust in Him to guide you and lead you in His truth. Place your hope in Him because He will never let you down.

Father,

You can see all the obstacles in my path before I encounter them. You are there to help guide me past them. Sometimes, you will guide me around them; sometimes, you will help me bypass them altogether, and sometimes, you will guide me through them. Help me place my hope in you as you direct me where I am supposed to be. Amen.

Struggling and Stumbling but Standing Firm

"The Lord directs the steps of the godly. He delights in every detail of their lives. Though they stumble, they will never fall, for the Lord holds them by the hand."
Psalm 37:23-24 NLT

God created us for fellowship with Him. He has always wanted to have a relationship with us and be there for us when we need Him. He is God, but He is also our Heavenly Father. He cares about our lives and what we go through. He wants us to delight in Him. But what does it mean to delight in Him?

To delight in God is to look forward to spending time with him. When we get up in the morning, we should want to spend a few minutes of quiet time with God. Sometimes, it may be reading over a verse that speaks to you or what you may be going through. Other times, you may pour your heart out to Him because you are completely overwhelmed and don't know what to do. Sometimes, you may not say anything at all, just simply listening for Him to speak to you in His still, small voice.

When we delight in the Lord, He listens. I can't explain it, but I can tell the difference in my countenance and God's spirit in me when I delight in Him vs. when I just go through the motions. You know what I mean by going through the motions. We've all done it. We read through our devotion in two seconds, and none of it sinks in because our minds are focused on all the other tasks we have to accomplish. Then we say a short general prayer, again with our mind on everything but God, and we jump up and check the box in our head to feel good that we had our quiet time with God. Meanwhile, He is up in heaven scratching his head and wondering why we even sat down because we clearly weren't there to spend time with Him.

When we delight in Him, it doesn't mean we have to spend an hour praying and reading our Bible, but the time we do spend with Him is focused on Him alone. We should close our eyes and imagine we are in the very throne room of God. We should thank Him for all the ways He blesses us. We can pour our hearts out to Him over what troubles us. Sometimes, in my quiet times, I can't even speak. I literally just cry out to Him because He already knows why I am upset. Many times, I have a Bluetooth speaker playing at home, and I play Christian music through it, just worshiping Him. That is what He means by delighting in Him. We meet Him where we are, tears streaming down our faces or joy radiating all over. When I spend my time delighting in Him, I feel a closeness to Him that can't be explained. The more quality time I spend with Him, the more I feel Him opening my mind and giving me a clear picture of the path He wants me on.

Our verse today says, "The Lord makes firm the steps of the one who delights in Him." What is the difference between a firm step and a shaky, unsure step? A firm step is confident in its direction, while the other is clueless.

The second part of this verse doesn't say we won't have

problems. It says, "Though he may stumble, he will not fall." We aren't immune to trials. We will have them. All people, Christians and non-Christians alike, will have trials and hard times. The difference is that we have the Lord holding our hands. We may get sick. We may have heartaches. We may have suffering. But we have hope, too. We have the God of the Universe holding our hands. Aren't you glad to know we can't fall from His grasp?

Moment to Reflect:

- ♥ Do you take time to delight in the Lord each day?
- ♥ Have you stopped through the midst of your heartache and pain and just listened for God to speak to you?
- ♥ Do you have Godly prayer warriors lifting you up when you are struggling so you won't be so discouraged?
- ♥ Have you felt the hand of God in your life holding you up to keep you from falling?

I'm thankful that God doesn't sugarcoat His Scripture. He doesn't promise that everything will always be perfect or that we won't face struggles and overwhelming circumstances. All He wants is for us to delight in Him, trust him, and rely on Him. He wants us to have a relationship with Him. He doesn't want us to stumble, but when we do, He is there to offer his hand to catch us before we fall.

Father,

My steps are shaky without you. Help me to trust in you in every aspect of my life and delight in spending time with you. I pray that I will crave that fellowship with you and listen for your still, small voice to direct my steps. Help my steps be firm, as I trust in you to guide me. Help me to take your hand when you offer it so that even when I am in the midst of deep despair, you pull me up before I fall. Amen.

The Still Small Voice Still Guides Us

"Whether you turn to the right or to the left, your ears will hear a voice behind you, saying, 'This is the way; walk in it.'"
Isaiah 30:21

Why do we try to have a backup plan when God should be our only plan? When we try to figure things out on our own or go our own way rather than seek His help and His direction, we are showing Him we don't have faith that He can handle the situation. Today's verse references a time when Jewish leaders didn't consult God, and instead of relying on God alone, they chose a backup plan.

Big mistake.

God was the Jews' security, but instead of trusting Him alone, they went and formed a treaty with Egypt to protect them from the Assyrians. God's exact words in Isaiah 30:1-2 are: "'Woe to the obstinate children,' declares the Lord, 'to those who carry out plans that were not mine, forming an alliance, but not by my Spirit, heaping sin upon sin; who go down to Egypt without consulting me; who look for help to Pharaoh's protection, to Egypt's shade for refuge.'"

Do you know what is so ironic about the people trusting in military strength from Egypt? Assyria was greater in military strength than Egypt! Not only did the Israelites not have enough faith to trust God to protect them, but the people they turned to could not protect them.

Despite their lack of faith, God had mercy on them. God may still discipline us when we make mistakes, but He always loves us and provides guidance where we need it. In verse 21, when He says, "Whether you turn to the right or to the left, your ears will hear a voice behind you, saying, 'This is the way, walk in it,'" it paints a clear picture of His willingness to guide us to where we need to be.

There may be times as a mom when you are unsure which direction to take. Whether it's in your personal life, your job, your children, friendships, relationships, etc., always know that God is there behind you. It is amazing to me that He desires to give us direction and guidance if we just ask Him. The God of all creation longs to show you compassion. His still, small voice will direct us in the way we should go. Sometimes, we just need to be still enough to hear it.

Moment to Reflect:

- ♥ Do you listen for God's voice as you make decisions?
- ♥ Have you gone to others for help as a backup plan in case God doesn't come through for you?
- ♥ Are you right in your relationship with God so when He does speak... Do you hear Him?
- ♥ Can you think of ways God has led you in your life as a mom that were a blessing when, at the time, you didn't realize He was protecting you?

I am so thankful that with God, we don't need a backup plan. If we seek His guidance and listen for His voice, we won't need to call in reinforcements.

Father,

Help me to have complete confidence in you in every aspect of my life. It is human nature to want to doubt and have unbelief, but as a Christian mom, I must have faith. Guard my heart and help me to be still so I can hear your still, small voice as you stand behind me and direct me in the way I am supposed to go. May I walk in it so I will be able to help my children walk in it. Amen.

Wisdom

"Be strong enough to stand alone, smart enough to know
when you need help, and brave enough to ask for it."
–Ziad K. Abdelnour

Stay Clear of Harm and Walk with the Wise

---

*"Walk with the wise and become wise, associate with fools
and get in trouble."*
Proverbs 13:20 NLT

God encourages us to be careful with whom we surround ourselves. The people we spend the most time with usually have the most influence on us. If the people closest to us are not walking with God, their influence could harm our character, our testimonies, and our lives. This verse in Proverbs 13:20 can also apply to our children. We should pray for them to walk with the wise.

When the verse says, "Walk with the wise and become wise," it does not mean wisdom by the world's standards but rather wisdom according to God's standards. God gives wisdom to those who fear Him. Fearing God doesn't mean being afraid of Him. It means having a healthy respect for Him and His power. Proverbs 9:10 says, "The fear of the Lord is the beginning of wisdom, and the knowledge of the Holy One is understanding." If you have knowledge, you have firsthand experience. This tells me if I want to have wisdom, I need to make an effort to *know* Him, *worship* Him, obey Him, and surround myself with like-minded people. So, when He says, "Walk with the wise and become wise," He is saying to walk with those who have a healthy fear and reverence for God. Walk with those who walk with Him and live by His word.

If you are unsure if you are walking with the wise, ask God for discernment to give you the wisdom to surround yourself with those who are wise. Throughout my life as a mom, I have tried to be part of Bible studies, volunteer at VBS, find a small group to plug into with couples who have kids around our kids' ages or older, participate in parenting classes our church offered on Wednesday nights, and attend Christian seminars with leaders who are wise and have already been through what I am struggling with. The reason I actively seek these opportunities is because the people in them and the people teaching them have wisdom. They already have been through many of the things I struggle with as a mom. It helps to get wise Christian counsel from those who have experienced what I haven't yet.

Be careful where you go for advice and wisdom. You need to pray and ask God to help you find the wise people to help you, as not everyone will give you the wise counsel you seek. Ask Him to guard you against "fools," who may lead you away from Him and into harm. If you are surrounded by people who are not following God's Word and don't have a healthy fear of the Lord, be very careful. You could be headed for destruction. Pray for your children to have discernment as they form friendships, too. The influence they have in their lives is just as important as yours.

This world has many who are "foolish" and lack the wisdom to live and make good decisions. We need to pray that God would use us to point them to the truth, to the wisdom of His Word, and to His love. We need to influence them without being influenced by them.

Pray for God to give you the strength to make the tough calls with friendships that could be leading you away from Him. Pray for Him to bring friends into your life and into your children's lives who will lead you toward Christ. Pray for Him to give you the courage and conviction to stand up for what's right in a world filled with wrong. Be the light to a world that needs it without being part of the world.

Moment to Reflect:

- ♥ Are you walking with the wise daily? Are you encouraging your kids to do the same?
- ♥ Do you have friends who could be considered "foolish" and who are influencing you in a worldly way?
- ♥ Are you strengthening your relationship with God daily so you will be able to discern if there are changes you need to make in relationships? Are you praying for your kids to have discernment in relationships?
- ♥ Can you think of ways to be a light in this world and influence others in a positive way without being influenced in a way that brings harm?

Being a Christian today is tough. We are called to love everyone, but we still must be careful in our quest to reach others so that we don't lose ourselves in the process. Always seek wisdom from Christ as you make decisions and form friendships. Be the light without losing your own!

Father,

Help me to be wise as I live my life. Help me to be in your word and be strong in my faith so foolish companions do not easily influence me. Provide me with friendships that will lift you up, encourage me in my faith, and bring wisdom into my life. Help me to encourage my children to do the same. I pray that as I walk with the wise, I will be able to be the light for the ones who don't know you. Protect me from harm as I seek to point others to you! Amen.

When You Don't Know, Just Ask

"If any of you lacks wisdom, you should ask God, who gives generously to all without finding fault, and it will be given to you."
James 1:5

Have you ever made yourself sick trying to figure out what you were supposed to do when you were clueless? As moms, we have all been there. It's frustrating. It's exhausting. It's scary. How do you decide between two options? Which one is best?

Have you ever just stopped and asked God for wisdom? It's hard enough when you are making decisions for yourself, but when you need wisdom concerning your child, it is extremely tough. It shouldn't be so difficult. It sounds so simple, doesn't it? Just ask for help! Why are we afraid or too stubborn to ask God for wisdom in our circumstances? Maybe we have made bad choices in the past without God's help. Maybe we don't feel worthy. We could lack faith and not feel like He can help. It could possibly be that we feel our problems are insignificant to the God of the Universe.

This verse in James says otherwise. This verse says God cares. If we lack wisdom, we *should* ask God. Why? Because He gives generously, without finding fault. Even if we have messed up in the past and have not asked for help, He still wants to help us now.

How does He give us wisdom? We can always glean wisdom through His Word. He gives us Scriptures, entire passages, and parables to help us learn a lesson or guide us in a certain way. He also uses Godly people in our lives. It could be a mentor, a parent, a friend, a counselor, a pastor, a teacher, or even a co-worker. God brings people into our lives and allows them to share their experience, testimonies, or advice so we may gain wisdom through the lives of others. My mom was able to share her Godly wisdom with my husband and me when we were deciding where God wanted us to move. God used her devotions and prayers to speak directly to us with a Scripture verse that told us word for word what He wanted us to do!

He can also speak to us in that still, small voice and nudge us in a certain direction with His Holy Spirit. We may not be able to see the Holy Spirit, but He is a powerful guide to direct us in the way we should go. He can be your conscience and your guide. He is literally Jesus speaking to you in your heart to lead you! Listen when He speaks.

The next time you have a decision to make and you don't know what to do...ask for wisdom. Just wait and see how generously God gives it!

Moment to Reflect:

- ♥ Have you ever felt defeated because you did not know which choice to make?
- ♥ Are you stressing and making yourself sick because you have no idea which decision to make?
- ♥ Are you sure you are getting advice from Christian sources who will influence you in the way God wants you to go?
- ♥ Can you be an influence on someone else who may need to make a decision?

Every day, we are bombarded with decisions. Some are easy, but some make us stressed because they could impact major aspects of our lives and our children's lives. We can worry and literally make ourselves sick, or we can seek God's wisdom through His Word, His people, prayer, and listening to His Holy Spirit. Sometimes, all you have to do is ask!

Father,

I struggle sometimes when I have a decision to make. I weigh all my options, but sometimes I don't consult you for your advice. Forgive me for not coming to you first for wisdom to help me make my decisions. Please bring people along my path that can provide me with the wisdom I need to make the decision that keeps me in your will. Give me scripture to confirm my decision and Godly mentors I can pray with as I seek to make the right choice. Thank you for giving me wisdom generously when I ask. Amen.

Pursue Wisdom Like a Priceless Treasure

"My son, if you accept my words and store up my commands within you, turning your ear to wisdom and applying your heart to understanding, indeed, if you call out for insight and cry aloud for understanding, and if you look for it as for silver and search for it as for hidden treasure, then you will understand the fear of the Lord and find the knowledge of God. For the Lord gives wisdom; from his mouth come knowledge and understanding."
Proverbs 2:1-6

Does anyone remember the movie "Goonies"? I used to love that movie. This group of kids, who were about to lose their homes, discovered an ancient map in an attic and went through a crazy ordeal to try to find the hidden treasure and save their town. They used the wisdom of some who knew Spanish with the musical skills of another to understand the ancient map. They searched for understanding and cried out for insight until they found the treasure they sought. King Solomon, who has been called the wisest man who ever lived, shared the verses in Proverbs 2:1-6 to show us how to value wisdom and treasure understanding so we can know the fear of the Lord.

If we take it verse by verse, just like the Goonies read the map line by line, they become easier to understand. In the first verse, when it says, "If you accept my words and store up my commands within you," what does that mean? If you accept God's words, you believe them to be true. If you store up His commands within you, you realize how important His commands are, and you save them in a special place in your heart. Not only should we store up His commands in our hearts, but we should also teach them to our children so they can store them in their hearts. Kids learn from a young age. When you read verses to them each day or write a verse on a bulletin board in a playroom or pin an index card or post it to a bathroom mirror or the fridge, they see that verse every day. It soaks in.

In the second verse that says to turn your ear to wisdom and apply your heart to understanding, the Psalmist exhorts us to receive His wisdom and apply it to our hearts. We can do this with every choice we make. We must choose to pursue wisdom every day. As a mom, I try to find moms who have already been through the stage I am going through with my kids. These moms may have struggles, but they also may have successes! I want to hear what worked for them and what they would have done differently. I have the chance to use their wisdom and insight to help me make better decisions concerning what I do or how I parent my kids.

Verse 3 mentions us calling out for insight and crying aloud for understanding. When we cry out for something, we are telling God we want it! It's okay for our kids to see us seeking help from God. Let them see you pray. Let them see you ask for guidance. God's wisdom is priceless, and our children should know that we treasure it.

Have you ever lost a piece of jewelry? I lost a diamond out of my engagement ring when my kids were little, and we crawled on the floor and looked under rugs and blankets, searching for it. If we look for wisdom as we would look for a diamond we lost or for any hidden treasure, we show God how much it means to us. God wants us to seek wisdom like we would seek the most precious stones and most valuable gems. That is how priceless wisdom is.

We are this priceless to God. In Luke 15:8-10, the parable of the lost coin shows us a woman who loses a coin that is very valuable to her. She lights a lamp so she can see and sweeps her house to look in every corner until she finds it. She is so excited that she calls her neighbors and friends to celebrate with her. In this story, we are like the lost coin, and Jesus is the one searching for us. We are valuable to Him, and He will never give up looking for us because He doesn't want us to be lost. When God does find us, all of Heaven rejoices because we are special to God.

If we do all these things, He says, then we will understand the fear of the Lord and find the knowledge of God. It doesn't come easily. We must pursue, want, seek, and cry out for God's wisdom.

Moment to Reflect:

- ♥ Do you think of wisdom as a priceless treasure to seek and keep safe?
- ♥ Are you choosing to seek wisdom in the choices you make? (Not just the big choices, but the everyday choices that define who you are?)
- ♥ Do you cry out to God for understanding and insight when you are confused or when you do not know what to do? Do your children see how much you value God's wisdom in your life?

Solomon was a very wise king. If you read about him, you know he wasn't born that way. He asked God for wisdom. He sought it because He knew its true value. The knowledge of God is a priceless treasure, and He is willing to share it with us if we ask Him. How much do you value wisdom in your life?

Father,

You gave Solomon the wisdom that made him the wisest man who ever lived. All he had to do was ask for it. Lord, I know how valuable your wisdom is, and I want to seek it and treasure it with all my heart. I want my children to treasure it, too. Your wisdom can help me make good choices in my life. Your wisdom can help me to be who I am meant to be and keep me from making bad choices. Help me always to seek your wisdom in every aspect of my life and never doubt its value. Help me to show my children what a treasure it is. Amen.

The Tamer of Stallions

"But the wisdom that comes from heaven is first of all pure;
then peace-loving, considerate, submissive, full of mercy and
good fruit, impartial and sincere."
James 3:17

Have you ever seen a wild horse being tamed? It is a process because you have to handle the horse gently, not roughly like its nature. You do all the normal things and tend to his needs (feed him, pet him, groom him), and then he will slowly grow to like you as he gets used to you. As the horse begins to trust you, he will allow you to ride him because he has no fight left. There is nothing for him to fight. This method uses wisdom in knowing a wild horse and how he responds to get the result we want.

We are like wild stallions with God sometimes. He has so much wisdom to give us, but first, He meets our needs and gains our trust. He is considerate and full of mercy when we go against Him. He sincerely wants what is best for us. We finally get to a point when we realize His motives are pure, and His "taming" allows us to have a more fulfilled life than one on our own.

Do your children see you as wise? Some view wisdom as merely being smart or brilliant, but it is so much more. The wisdom that comes from God incorporates so many characteristics into one. The world is driven by greed and selfishness, just like the wild stallion is driven to run and be wild. Without Godly wisdom, this world is filled with evil and hurt as people step over others to get what they want. When we reject selfishness and trust God to provide for what we need, our motives become pure and peaceful, striving to put others first instead of ourselves. This peaceful nature, just like taming the stallion, reduces conflict and makes us more considerate of others and better moms because we don't allow anger to take control. If you have more than one child, you will constantly be called on to reduce conflict. Godly wisdom helps us handle this in a way that speaks volumes to our kids, making us more willing to listen and be open to discussion. As we strive for peace, our attitudes are naturally calmer instead of defensive. We aren't weak or cowardly, but we are willing to see another's viewpoint or compromise as long as we don't compromise our values and beliefs.

Wisdom goes hand in hand with mercy. When God gives us wisdom, He allows us to be compassionate and show forgiveness, even if someone doesn't deserve it. As parents, we have shown mercy to our kids many times when they could have been punished or disciplined for their actions. Sometimes discipline is necessary, but there are times when wisdom tells us that mercy is the better choice. This helps them to see that God has mercy on us many times when we don't deserve it.

At the end of James 3:17, it mentions the wisdom that comes from heaven is full of good fruit. Have you ever heard the phrase, "You will know them by their fruit"? This phrase is from Matthew 7:16 and talks about how good trees produce good fruit and bad trees produce bad fruit. If we are full of good fruit, that means we show in our actions that we are growing in the Lord, and others can see Godly characteristics in our everyday lives. When we are impartial, our wisdom allows us to treat everyone equally and show the love of Christ in all we do. Lastly, James mentions that the wisdom from heaven is sincere. This means we are genuine, not showy or fake or trying to be someone we are not. We are who God created us to be.

Moment to Reflect:

- ♥ When your children see you, do they see any of the eight characteristics listed in James 3:17?
- ♥ As you raise your children, do you find yourself peaceful and considerate or combative and rude?
- ♥ Does the world see mercy and submissiveness as you handle conflict, or are you living without God's wisdom in handling situations?
- ♥ Does your social media reflect the real you, or are you living in the worldly view of insincerity?

This world has many brilliant people who make it a better place. You don't have to be brilliant to be wise and make a difference. Are you asking God for wisdom? Do you see some of the characteristics that come naturally when we use God's wisdom in our lives and in our parenting?

Father,

I value the wisdom that comes from you. I know that it helps me to be more peaceful, kind, and considerate to others, but especially to my children. I want to handle conflict in a Godly way, and as I go throughout this life, I pray I will be full of mercy and sincerity so others will know I am a child of yours. Help my children to see Christ in me as I seek your wisdom daily. Amen.

Build It On The Rock!

> "Therefore everyone who hears these words of mine and puts them into practice is like a wise man who built his house on the rock. The rain came down, the streams rose, and the winds blew and beat against that house; yet it did not fall, because it had its foundation on the rock."
> Matthew 7:24-25

Our family had our house built, and I saw from the beginning how the ground was cleared and the foundation was laid. I don't know the first thing about construction and built-to-code and all the rules and regulations required to build a structure of any kind. It is amazing to see a house built from start to finish and see how much time goes into laying the foundation. Before any walls could go up, before any floors, cabinets, or doors could be put in, the foundation had to be laid.

The kind of foundation Matthew is talking about is the kind I want for myself and my children. I want them to listen to God's words and put them into practice. I want them to have a firm grip on their beliefs so that when they have teachers, friends, coaches, classmates, and co-workers who try to entice them with worldly temptations or false teachings, they will know where they stand. They will stand for Jesus!

Matthew 7:24-25 compares putting God's words into action to building a house on a rock. When your foundation is on a solid rock, it is firm. When we seek God's wisdom and use it to build our own lives, our spiritual foundation will be secure. This is such a valuable lesson to teach our children. You are never too young to start building your foundation on Christ!

I did a little digging and looked up companies that specialize in foundation repair. I found many similarities between building our houses on solid foundations and building our lives on "solid rock" (Jesus). In one article, someone asked if you could build a house without a foundation. The answer was yes, if you realize it is not designed to last! The writer detailed certain things you could look for that would indicate your foundation was not structurally sound. If your home had settling, sinking, large cracks in walls and floors, gaps in exterior window frames, separation of cabinets from the wall, etc., it was not structurally sound.

One site talked about how important it was to build on a solid foundation because, during certain seasons, the temperature changes, and the ground expands and contracts. This can cause instability if your house is not built on a rock that is solid. Your entire foundation could be shaky. As Christians, if we don't build our lives on the firm foundation of Christ, we will experience settling instead of standing strong. There will be cracks in our ability to withstand pressure and temptations, gaps in our quiet times and prayer life, separation of ourselves and Christian friends that can encourage us in our faith, and the list goes on. It is amazing how much our foundation matters in our walk with Christ. Our kids need to know that when we take these Scriptures and these lessons God gives us throughout the Bible, and we hide them in our hearts, and we apply them to our own lives, God builds His foundation in our hearts, and it continues to get stronger as we grow in Him.

I want my legacy to last. I want what I build in my spiritual life to mean something. I want to be firm in my faith, not shaky.

The foundation I build now for my children will set a strong example for their faith to grow and build their own strong foundation in the future – a foundation that will not fall.

Moment to Reflect:

- ♥ Do you put God's words of wisdom into practice daily?
- ♥ Have you built your life on a firm foundation in Christ to help withstand the storms that may come your way?
- ♥ Have you seen any examples of settling, sinking, cracks, gaps, or separation in your own life that suggests your foundation may need repair?
- ♥ Can you help anyone else who looks like their foundation may be struggling?

As I read these verses in Matthew and think about my own foundation in Christ, I pray that I will take the wisdom He has shared with us in His Word and apply it to my everyday life so I can withstand any winds and storms coming my way.

Father,

There is so much wisdom in all your scripture. Your word is not an old book of events that happened ages ago. It is living and breathing advice straight from you to us and is filled with insight and first-hand knowledge. Help me to realize how important it is to build my life on you as my rock. I pray that I will always look to you for insight into how to make my foundation stronger. I want to build it to last. I want my children to have a legacy of a solid foundation of faith. Amen.

You Are Never Too Old to Grow

"And Jesus grew in wisdom and stature,
and in favor with God and man."
Luke 2:52

This verse in Luke was the last line of my son's favorite book when he was little. The book portrayed Jesus as a little boy on his knees praying beside his bed. My son was about the age of the young Jesus portrayed in the book, and it made me smile that even Jesus grew spiritually as He grew up. I would always pray as I read the book to my son, asking God for him to grow in wisdom as he grew up, too.

We know that Jesus came to earth as a human, and because of that, He may have given up certain privileges that came with being God. Jesus had to learn to walk and talk, and He grew up learning Scripture just like the other kids His age. There is a gap in the Biblical narrative between His birth and age 12, and then another gap between age 12 and when He started His ministry at age 30. Regardless of these gaps, we do know that Jesus grew spiritually, and knowledge of God's word helped Him grow in wisdom as well.

As Jesus grew in stature, He also grew in favor with God. How do you grow in favor with God? You grow spiritually. So, as Jesus grew physically, He also grew spiritually. He learned the Scriptures, kept them in His heart, and applied them to His life. At age 30, Jesus was known as a great teacher. To teach others, He had to continue to learn and increase His knowledge. As He taught and learned, He not only gained favor with God, but He also gained favor with men. He was respected as a teacher, and people came in large crowds to hear Him teach.

What can we take away from this short but powerful verse? We can realize that we are never too old to grow in wisdom. Spiritual growth is a lifelong journey, and regardless of age, there is always room to deepen your faith. As you grow older, the wisdom gained from years of life experiences can contribute significantly to your spiritual development. Aging often involves challenges like illness and loss, which can become profound opportunities for spiritual growth as you examine your purpose and beliefs.

As we age, the desire to leave a meaningful legacy becomes more prominent. Spiritual growth can play a crucial role in achieving this goal. Additionally, with the passage of time, we come to appreciate the preciousness of each moment and strive to live our faith more fully. Whether young or old, we all have the opportunity to enrich our lives by continuing to grow spiritually.

The more we study Scripture and apply it to our lives, the more we will gain favor with God. Even Jesus grew in wisdom, so if He can grow in it, I know we can, too!

Moment to Reflect:

- ♥ What are you doing to grow spiritually? How are you helping your children to grow spiritually?
- ♥ Do you study Scripture and apply it to all aspects of your life?
- ♥ Are you consistently trying to learn and grow in your walk with God, regardless of how old you are?

We may be grown physically, but spiritually, we should always be growing. Jesus showed us that He could grow in wisdom, even though He is the son of God. That gives me hope that if I read His word and apply it to my life, I can grow in wisdom as well.

Lord Jesus,

You set such a great example growing up! You showed us that reading God's word is important, but it is even more important to apply it to our lives. I want to grow in wisdom and be closer to you every day. Help me to create time to study your word and apply it to every aspect of my life. Amen.

Seek Your Wisdom from Above, Not This World

"Who is wise and understanding among you? Let him show it by their good life, by deeds done in the humility that comes from wisdom."
James 3:13

If you had to make a choice where one outcome led to safety and the other led to destruction, which would you choose? It seems obvious, right? Sometimes, this is the difference between Godly wisdom and worldly wisdom. We must be careful who we seek our wisdom from because it could lead to very different outcomes. Godly wisdom is pure, gracious, good, and sincere, while worldly wisdom leads to selfish ambition, boastfulness, conceit, pride, and jealousy, which are characteristics of this world.

As you strive to become closer to God and build a firm foundation in Him, you will recognize the characteristics of those around you who have Godly wisdom. They will have a calm demeanor and be peacemakers. They won't be conceited or prideful but humble in spirit, always seeking God's will in every situation and full of mercy. When we have Godly wisdom in our lives, it is demonstrated through our actions and decisions.

Wisdom is an honor that those with worldly knowledge put on a pedestal. It often makes their actions selfish and egotistical. They tend to act boastfully, and sometimes, they cause dissension with their conceited attitudes and actions. Godly wisdom is sincere and gracious and promotes peace and mercy rather than dissension and strife.

I can tell in my own life by how I handle certain situations whether I have been getting too much worldly wisdom or whether I have been seeking Godly wisdom. When I start feeling prideful, jealous, or self-centered, it's a sign that I've allowed worldly wisdom to impact me negatively. I notice that I become more self-focused, unforgiving, and selfish, prioritizing my own needs over those of others. James 3:13 says, "Let him show [wisdom] by his good life, by deeds done in the humility that comes from wisdom." True Godly wisdom gives you humility rather than boastfulness. It helps you choose graciousness instead of selfishness and pride.

As a mom who is trying to raise my children to love Jesus and honor Him in everything they do, I need to seek Godly wisdom and surround myself with Godly influencers who can pour into me the love of Christ and help me to seek Him always. When you think about this verse and you read, "Who is wise and understanding among you?" Let it be yourself. Know who to look for that has purity, graciousness, sincerity, and peace. It will be obvious. Is your wisdom from the world or from above? It makes a difference!

Moment to Reflect:

- ♥ What do your actions say about the wisdom you have in your life?
- ♥ Is your wisdom from this world, or is it from above?
- ♥ What are the traits of those you know with Godly wisdom versus the traits of someone with worldly wisdom?

As a mom, I want to be wise, but I want to be sure I am seeking the wisdom from above. My influences should be godly, and my actions should speak for themselves. I pray they are peaceful and full of humility.

Lord Jesus,

There are many people on this earth who are wise beyond belief, but their actions are full of pride, selfishness, and boastfulness. I seek the wisdom that comes from you. Let my actions be humble and let me be gracious, and seek peace in everything I do. I pray my life always reflects the goodness of your mercy. Amen.

God's Will

"Being a mother is learning about the strengths you didn't
know you had... and dealing with fears
you didn't know existed."
–Linda Wooten

DAY 36

Silence Them with Sweetness

"For it is God's will that by doing good you should silence the ignorant talk of foolish men."
1 Peter 2:15

More than ever before, the media seems to focus on bringing mistakes into the open, especially those of Christians in high levels of authority and power. When we make bad choices and we don't "do good," as 1 Peter 2:15 says, we set ourselves up for scrutiny from unbelievers. In other words, they are looking for us to mess up. They are waiting for us to make a wrong move, to say something we shouldn't, or to do something that goes against the values we hold dear.

Peter tells us that it is by God's will that He wants us to "do good" so that others will not be able to give Christians a bad name. What is God's will? In the Greek language, the word "will" is *Thelema*, which is desire or what one wants. God's "desire" is for us to "do good." The word "good" in the Greek language is *agathos*, which means the good that acts for the benefit of others. God's desire is for us to act for the benefit of others. We hurt our witness when we don't "do good." If our actions in everyday life are the same as non-Christians, how are they supposed to tell the difference of Christ in our lives?

There should be a difference. How we act at our children's games and how we act at parties or other events matters. Our TV and movie choices, music preferences, words, decisions, company, treatment of others, and actions should reflect Christ within us.

When 1 Peter 2:15 mentions foolish men, that could be anyone who believes certain views about Christians without knowing what they are really like. The ignorant talk could refer to the accusations they throw out toward Godly people because they simply don't know any better. How can we help them to silence these accusations? Simply, "do good."

As Christians, we need to "do good" in our everyday lives so others watching us will not be able to say anything bad about Christians. How we act and react affects others' opinions about God and who He is. I don't want to portray God as mean, judgmental, rude, prideful, selfish, arrogant, or boastful through my actions.

As you go about your day, whether you are at work or with your kids out in public, be conscious of how you are acting. Make sure you are "doing good." God didn't say to be perfect. He just said, "do good." You can do good in little ways. I have put my neighbor's trash can up before or fixed dessert and scooped some out to take to a neighbor or friend. I try to be friendly to others when I go to the grocery store or run errands. I bite my tongue sometimes at my son's games when the referee makes a bad call because I know that could ruin my witness. I am conscious of the music I listen to, and most of the time, it is from a Christian radio station (occasionally country). We always tip well at restaurants and try to get to know our waiters because you never know when you can make a difference in their lives. We have enjoyed getting to know several at restaurants we frequent, and sometimes, it opens up opportunities to share Christ. We can all strive to have a little more "good" in our lives.

Moment to Reflect:

- ♥ Can others who are non-Christians tell I am a Christian by my actions?
- ♥ Do I lead others away from or toward Christ by how I live?
- ♥ Are there changes I can make in my day-to-day activities that can strengthen my witness as a Christian?

Who knew that just by being good, we can silence those who may be against us? Sometimes, they are against us because they are ignorant and have a false view of how Christians really are. Don't be the Christian that gives others a bad name. Try to "do good" so you can be in God's will.

Lord Jesus,

I never realized how many others look to me to see how I am living and what choices I am making. Help me to be strong in my faith so that when I am tempted to make a wrong choice, I will choose to "do good." I want to be in your will. Help me, through my actions, to silence those who are ignorant of the ways of Christianity. Let them see you through everything I do and say. Amen.

For Such a Time as This

"For if you remain silent at this time, relief and deliverance for the Jews will arise from another place, but you and your father's family will perish. And who knows but that you have come to a royal position for such a time as this?"
Esther 4:14

How many of you have dreamed of being a princess? We have grown up with fairytales of Cinderella, who was treated as a servant, managed to capture the prince's heart, and became royalty. The story of Esther is similar, but it is no fairytale. This true story, straight from the Bible, happened to a young Jewish girl who captured the heart of the King and became his queen when the Jews needed her most. The king in this story had already banished his first queen because she refused to obey an order. He decided to choose a new queen from a multitude of young girls from all the provinces in his kingdom, and he chose Esther.

The king gave a man named Haman a seat of honor higher than all the other nobles. All the officials knelt and paid him honor except for Mordecai, Esther's cousin. This angered Haman, and when he found out Mordecai was a Jew, he devised a plan to destroy all the Jews. He tricked the king to

155

gain approval for his plan, had the king seal the orders with his signet ring, and then had the orders delivered to all the provinces. These orders were to kill all the Jews on a certain day of a certain month.

Mordecai learned about the orders and went to Esther for help. No one knew Esther was a Jew. She was in a very scary position as queen. In those days, if you went before the king without being summoned, it could result in death. If the king realized she was a Jew, she could be killed with all the others. She prayed and fasted as she tried to figure out what to do for her people. Mordecai's response to her fear was this verse in Esther 4:14. If she remained silent, deliverance would come from another place, but what if she was in her position for that specific reason?

How many times have we been in a position where we were scared and didn't know what to do? I may not be royalty or an international agent helping the government stop plots against high-level officials, but I am a mom to three kids who depend on me! Facing situations where we, as moms, need to address issues with other parents or adults about our child—or another child—can be intimidating. We might also have the opportunity to share Jesus with a fellow parent from our child's team or class, and their reaction is uncertain. Additionally, we may find ourselves in a position to offer a safe home for a child in need, and we must be willing to be obedient to what God calls us to do. We were blessed to share our home with several different foster children. Being a foster mom, responsible for other people's children, was scary but very rewarding. God will find a way to accomplish His will, but sometimes He has put us in a specific position "for such a time as this."

Esther had the courage to confront the king, and as a result, Haman was punished, and the Jews were saved. Will we have the courage to do what God needs us to do as part of His will? God has gifted each of us with different talents and abilities. Motherhood encompasses many different roles and responsibilities. We are thrown into many scenarios as a mom, and it's our job to navigate them all, knowing where God wants to use us. You may be a nurse or doctor with medical training you could use on a mission trip or at a local clinic. Some of you may have backgrounds in education and could shape minds every day. Others of you may be great with numbers and find ways to save your company money or create an efficient budget for your family. Some may have people on church or school committees who need encouragement and reassurance of Jesus' love for them. No matter where you are, God has placed you in a position to be of service. We all have different ways we can touch people's lives if we choose to be obedient. You may be the one put in *your* position "for such a time as this!"

Moment to Reflect:

- ♥ Can you think of a time that God has allowed you to be part of His plan?
- ♥ Is your relationship with Christ close enough to hear His voice when He asks you to step out in faith?
- ♥ What position has God placed you in? How can you make a difference?
- ♥ Would you be like Esther if God called you to speak up, or would you be silent?
- ♥ What gifts has God graced you with to point others to Jesus?

I am so amazed by Esther and the bravery she showed in the face of possible death. God allowed her to become queen, but she didn't take the position lightly. Even in her high rank, she was scared to do what needed to be done. She could have been silent, but she chose to bravely speak up. As mothers,

God has placed all of us in a position to make a difference. I pray that I will have the courage to act and allow Him to use me to accomplish His will.

Lord Jesus,

You allow us to have certain positions to reach more people for the greater good. Help me to stay close to you and listen to your still, small voice so I will hear when you call me to do something. Help me to have the faith that I need and the courage that it takes to make a difference for your kingdom. Help me to be like Esther in a world full of Hamans! Amen.

DAY 38

No Room for Grey

"Do not conform to the pattern of this world, but be transformed by the renewing of your mind. Then you will be able to test and approve what God's will is – his good, pleasing and perfect will."
Romans 12:2

Short skirts, crop tops, baggy jeans, skinny jeans, flats, boots, animal prints, and stripes are some of many fashion trends over the years that have influenced us to wear the latest fad, whether it was appropriate or not. Entertainment such as movies, TV shows, and videos have become more inclusive of worldly standards. We line up for the popcorn and stream popular shows that don't depict the values we are supposed to live by.

We worry about peer pressure for our kids, but adults can experience peer pressure too. We are pressured to have the right job, drive a certain car, have a certain size house, shop at certain stores, go on certain vacations, etc. Fashion trends, entertainment, and peer pressure from all angles are all subtle ways Satan gets us to conform to this world a little at a time. As Christians, we are held to a higher standard. We weren't meant to blend in and not be noticed. If we choose to live how

God wants us to live, we will stand out. That's not a bad thing, but it is definitely the road less traveled, and it takes courage to be different.

Some of the stances we must take as moms won't win us popularity contests. It's hard to stand up for what is right when everyone else is choosing worldly values. Have you ever driven by a neighborhood of homes, and they all look exactly the same? The same floor plan, and the same paint color, same trim color, same door, and same garage doors, etc.? It's hard to tell any of them apart. None of them stand out because they are all alike. We may try to be the same as other moms because it's easier to go with the majority than to stand by ourselves. We don't want to be the mom who has an issue with a movie, a problem with a curfew time, or second thoughts about a certain party. We want to let it slide sometimes, so we are like the other moms. But we aren't supposed to be the same. We're supposed to be set apart. This requires a change in behavior, and it's hard.

We need to align our will with God's. By choosing to think, listen, speak, see, and hear in ways that honor Him, we become better able to understand His will. This is not a one-time thing. This is a choice we have to make daily. As moms, we need a support system to build us up and stay connected to God so we won't be swayed and give in to peer pressure. I know how hard it is to want to see a new movie that has just come out, but when you read the reviews, it has 32 uses of a word you know God doesn't approve of. My husband and I have stopped a TV show right in the middle before when it had a scene we thought was inappropriate. I've had discussions with our daughter about certain outfits that I felt were inappropriate. We are constantly surrounded by the world's standards on how to live.

If we are transformed, then we are changed from what the world says is okay. We have allowed the Holy Spirit to renew our minds, which doesn't allow room for listening to certain songs, watching certain movies or shows, or going to certain places. I don't think of it as restrictive. I just consider it to be choosing a better option. The best way to know the options that are in God's will is to spend time with Him (prayer, devotion, listening, singing, reading His Word, etc.) The more time we spend with God and in His Word, the more confident we will be in our choices. When others see us living our lives, they should be able to tell by everything we do that we are Christians. We may not have as many choices as the world, but the choices we make will change the world for the better. We can dress trendy, watch great shows, and listen to great music without compromising our values! We have an opportunity to show the world a better way. Let's show them that different can be better!

Moment to Reflect:

- ♥ Can you think of a situation you have been in when you had to make a choice about whether to go the world's way or God's way?
- ♥ Do you put certain things in categories or gray areas because you have allowed the world to conform your thinking regarding certain beliefs?
- ♥ Do you feel like the actions you choose and the choices you make can influence others to follow or reject Christ?
- ♥ Would you like to be closer to God so you can discern what His good and pleasing will is for your life?

It is not easy today to stand up for what is right when it seems like the entire world is against you. Being a Christian isn't easy, but it is extremely rewarding. The present-day culture has become accepting of things that Christians used to reject. We have chosen to be silent in a world that needs us to speak. Will you take a stand in your faith and be transformed to know

God's perfect will for you? I challenge you to grow in your faith so that you will be able to be the difference this world needs.

Lord Jesus,

Please forgive me for allowing myself to become lax in certain areas that I need to take a stand on. I pray that I will make more time for you daily and not only read your word but listen to your Holy Spirit as you speak to me. I pray you will help me to be strong in areas of weakness and to be able to take a stand for what is right and not give in to the gray areas of temptation. Help others to know I am a Christian by how I live my life day in and day out. I love you, Jesus. Amen.

DAY 39

One Minute at a Time

"Wait on the Lord; Be of good courage, and He shall strengthen your heart; Wait, I say, on the Lord!"
Psalm 27:14 NKJV

Sometimes, waiting is the hardest thing to do. All of us want our prayers answered immediately and don't understand when we get a delay. What is taking God so long? Why can't He just fix this? Maybe it would be better if I just tried to handle it myself. Have you ever been guilty of asking any of those questions? I know I have.

David is the author of most of the book of Psalms, and he went through a season when he was running for his life. Even though he was anxious, scared, and needed protection quickly, he trusted God enough to wait. He knew God had his best interests at heart and that God knew what was best for him even better than David did!

As parents, daughters, and sisters, we have all had situations where someone we loved needed help. Maybe you have had a parent who needed surgery, a sibling who had a tough diagnosis, or a child who was struggling. We want God to step in and handle it immediately so we don't have to suffer, hurt, trust, or be brave. Sometimes, God's answer is to wait.

My daughter hurt her leg in a basketball game. We took her to the ER thinking her leg could be sprained or broken, but she tore her ACL. The recovery from a broken leg would have been six weeks, but instead, it took almost a year for her leg to get strong enough to run track and cross country again. She had to have ice machines, physical therapy, crutches, and special showering procedures until her leg had time to heal. God used that time to make her stronger, and it allowed me to pamper her a little until she was back on her own two feet. While waiting for God to help her leg heal, we enjoyed making memories and spending quality time together that we wouldn't have had otherwise.

I will never understand God's timing, but I do know that it is always purposeful. You may be pushed to your absolute breaking point before you realize how strong you can be with God's help. When we have the courage to trust in Him and wait for Him, He strengthens us and our hearts to handle the situation we are in. It is never easy, but He allows us to rely on Him to carry us in times when we don't think we can make it on our own. Remember, if you are in a "waiting" position, God is still working behind the scenes. Use your wait as an opportunity to experience Him more and see how He strengthens you from within.

Moment to Reflect:

- ♥ Have you ever been forced to wait on God when you really needed an answer immediately?
- ♥ If you have had to wait on God to answer a prayer, could you see why God made you wait?
- ♥ Looking back on times in your life when your faith has been strengthened, was it when God answered immediately or when you had to go through a trial that tested every bit of strength you had?
- ♥ What has God shown you in times when you have had to wait on Him?

It is so hard in this world to sit back and wait for God to move in our lives when we are used to getting info at the click of a button, food in a drive-through or microwave, and calls from someone around the world in a matter of minutes. We don't like being inconvenienced or having to wait for anything. God's answers are not often immediate. Why does He make us wait? He has His reasons. He is God! He is all-powerful. All-knowing. He sees around the bend and knows what we need more than we do. Have the courage to trust Him and the patience to wait for His timing.

Lord Jesus,

I am terrible at waiting. I don't have a patient bone in my body. Please help me to trust in you to know what I need more than I do. I pray for courage as I wait for your perfect timing. Strengthen my faith and help me to get through this trial one minute at a time. Amen.

DAY 40

Thank You God

"Give thanks in all circumstances; for this is God's will for you in Christ Jesus."
1 Thessalonians 5:18

What is the first thing you think about when something bad happens? I'm talking about scenarios you pray never happen. Has your air conditioning ever gone out in the middle of July? Have you ever needed a plumber on a holiday weekend with guests coming? Has anyone ever had a sick child while you were on vacation? Have you experienced a job loss or a ton of unexpected expenses and wondered how God was going to provide? I'm guessing the first words out of your mouth for any of these situations were not, "Thank you, God" (unless you are extremely sarcastic). It's human nature to gripe and complain when circumstances are beyond our control. It stresses us out. It makes us angry. It can even make us bitter and resentful. We tend to expect that everything will go smoothly and that nothing unexpected will come up. When things don't go as planned, it's natural to lose our composure.

I wish I could be the person who sees the good in everything and never complains, but I'm not. It never fails that every time my husband travels for work, something breaks, one of our kids ends up at the doctor, the dogs end up at the Emergency Vet, or a light that isn't supposed to come on suddenly appears on the dashboard of my car. 1 Thessalonians 5:18 reminds me that we should be thankful in all things, even when we go through trials.

Why does it matter if we are thankful in hard circumstances? Think about it: if we are being thankful, what are we *not* doing? Chances are, we are not grumbling and complaining! It helps us keep a positive outlook, which can also be a good witness to nonbelievers who are watching us handle the situation. Our responses could have an eternal impact on those around us. Also, if we are being thankful, we are relying on God's strength to get us through. Instead of depending on ourselves, we are depending on God to make a way.

God's will for our lives is always better than anything we would choose, so start out small. Thank Him for the little things, and slowly, you will begin adding on the bigger things. Before long, your first response in times of trouble may be to give thanks instead of complaining. Your kids are watching you more than you realize. Your reaction can affect how they handle a situation as well. Looking back on some of my biggest trials, I realize those were the times my faith grew the most. God knows we don't like the circumstances, but He also knows what is best for us and can see how the trial will strengthen our faith.

Moment to Reflect:

- ♥ What is your first reaction when something bad happens?
- ♥ If you are one who becomes negative when bad things happen, how has that impacted the situation? Does it make it harder?
- ♥ Have you ever tried to be thankful in a situation or look for the positive, and if so, did it help to lessen the stress of the situation?
- ♥ How has God increased your faith in times of trial when you have chosen to thank Him, even when your world was caving in?

When bad things happen, sometimes the last thing we want to do is give thanks. Sometimes we want to scream. Sometimes we do! It takes so much faith to take a situation and say, "Okay, God, I don't understand what is happening, but I am going to thank you and ask you to help me through this." When you do that, your faith increases, and your reliance on God is strengthened. It's almost impossible to complain when you are being thankful. Try it!

Lord Jesus,

I don't understand why you have put me in this situation. My first instinct is to gripe and tell you all the reasons why it shouldn't be happening to me, but I won't. I choose to thank you even in this circumstance because I know you have a perfect plan, and I want to be in your will. I trust you to get me through this and I pray my faith is strengthened as I rely on you. I love you, Jesus. Amen.

More Like Jesus

"And what does the Lord require of you? To act justly and to love mercy and to walk humbly with your God."
Micah 6:8

So often, people think God has a lot of complicated rules for us when, really, He only desires that we do three things: act justly, love mercy, and walk humbly with Him.

Acting justly doesn't necessarily mean you need to be political. Being just is simply standing up for what is right, like speaking up when you see someone being bullied or mistreated in some way. I realized the importance of this when I got a call from another mom who told me my son had stood up to a bully for her own son. He stood up for what was right and didn't let others gang up and take advantage of someone who was singled out. I was proud of him for being willing to speak up. It's not easy to step forward and take a stand against the crowd. It takes character and strength. Having conversations with your kids about what they would do in certain situations can be helpful. Encouraging your kids to know what is right and choosing to do the right thing is a great way to build their character. Seeking justice for someone is a way to stand in the gap for those who can't do it themselves.

Thank goodness for mercy. None of us deserves it, but God gives it freely. If God can give mercy to us when we know we don't deserve it, shouldn't we love mercy enough to give it freely to others who probably don't deserve it either? When we seek to put others first instead of ourselves, we are more apt to show mercy to those even undeserving of it. It is the ultimate act of kindness that could open a door for you to share Christ or show the love of Christ to those who need Him. Their eternal life is worth more than your grudges and unforgiveness.

Lastly, but certainly not least, our instructions from Micah 6:8 include walking humbly with God. How do we achieve this? We learn from His example. Philippians 2:2-4 offers excellent guidance on humility and unity. It advises us to value others above ourselves, care about what matters to them, act selflessly, and avoid prioritizing personal ambitions over others. It's important to listen more than we speak, which requires a lot of self-control—something I know I need to improve on. Asking for help rather than trying to handle everything alone is another challenge for me; I struggle with this because I don't want to be a burden and tend to believe I can manage by myself. We should also strive to avoid pride and arrogance, be grateful rather than always wanting more, admit our mistakes, and support others instead of putting them down. Walking with God becomes difficult if we are constantly trying to move ahead of Him and do things on our own.

This verse in Micah provides so much instruction in so few words. If we could live by it, we would all be more like Jesus every day!

Moment to Reflect:

- ♥ Do you feel like Christians are held to a higher standard, and if so, what do you think it means to act justly?
- ♥ Are you able to show mercy even if it is someone who has badly wronged you?
- ♥ Do you see how showing someone mercy who probably doesn't deserve it could be a way to show them the love of Christ more than any other way?
- ♥ Is walking humbly harder than you realized after reading the list of examples? Could you make a conscious effort to walk humbly if it meant reaching someone for Jesus?

God desires for us to do these three things because He knows if we can act justly, love mercy, and walk humbly with Him, we will be living in His will for our lives. Standing up for what is right takes courage. Showing mercy when you would rather not forgive someone who has wronged you is hard. Kindness is one thing, but mercy is showing kindness to someone who doesn't deserve it. That's hard. Walking humbly takes a conscious effort on our part to put others first and not be selfish. It requires us to listen more and talk less. It forces us to put our pride aside and ask for help. God knew what He was doing when He spoke these desires to Micah. I encourage you to ask God to help you live out Micah 6:8. God empowers us to do these things, and it isn't through our own strength that we are sanctified. All we need to do is ask, and He comes alongside us to provide us with what we need.

Lord Jesus,

You don't ask for much, do you? You want me to possibly stand alone for what is right even if everyone around me is against me. You want to show mercy to those who don't deserve it. Lastly, you want me to set aside my pride, ask for help when I am used to doing things on my own, admit when I am wrong, and put others ahead of myself. There is no way I can do this without your help, Lord. I ask you to help me live out Micah 6:8 in everything I do. I know that if I can act justly, love mercy, and walk humbly with you, I can lead others to Christ and let them see you in me. Help me to be a good example of that Jesus. Amen

Pray with Expectations

"This is the confidence we have in approaching God: that if we ask anything according to his will, he hears us."
1 John 5:14

Have you ever prayed and then wondered if God really heard it? All of us have had times when we felt like our prayers weren't even making it past the ceiling in our room, much less into heaven. What a comfort to know that if we are asking God for something that is in His will, He hears us. 1 John 5:14 doesn't say God will answer according to how we think He should. It doesn't say that He will answer at the time we choose. It *does* say that if it is according to *His* will, He will hear it. The God of the universe hears *our* prayers.

Our perfect plans and desires may not be God's. Just because He doesn't respond according to our timing or in the way we expect doesn't mean He isn't looking out for our best interests! He has plans far greater than anything we could ask or imagine, and they unfold according to His will and timing.

I have prayed so hard for things in the past and would get so frustrated when I felt like God didn't answer. But He definitely did, and as I grew in faith, I was able to see that. I could see how He orchestrated events and brought people in my path when He was ready and when my heart was ready. I thought I knew best, but His plan was always better than anything I could have imagined. There were things I thought I really wanted to be part of in college – but I tried out and didn't make it. At the time, I was devastated. I didn't realize that not being part of those things freed me up to take a summer job, and *that* allowed me to meet the love of my life that I have been married to for over 26 years! God is so good!

God wants us to pray in faith, expecting Him to move. That is where confidence comes in. Don't ever doubt that God hears your prayers when you pray according to His will. What is according to His will? Usually, these are the hardest words to pray, surrendering our desires for how we want God to answer our prayer. We must surrender to His will and how He chooses to answer us. We must desire His will even more than what we desire. Pray with confidence that He is listening, and He will answer in His timing. After you pray, show your confidence in God by watching for His actions. He has His own way, but it is never a question of "if," but "when."

I encourage you to get a small, inexpensive journal and record your prayers. Write the date you first prayed each one and then always go back and write the date He answered them! Go back and look through that journal when you are sad or doubting whether He is listening, and see how many times He answered your prayers… according to His will. How many times was His will so much better than anything you could have imagined?

Moment to Reflect:

- ♥ Do you feel like you pray confidently to God, expecting Him to move?
- ♥ Are you praying according to God's will, or are you selfishly seeking your own desires instead of God's desires for your life?
- ♥ Have you seen God move in your prayer life and answer your prayers when you were praying according to His will?
- ♥ Do you keep a journal to write down your prayers so you can record when God answers them? That is praying with expectation!

I get so excited when I see God answer prayer. Sometimes, we doubt He can do it, and then when He does, we are amazed. We need to be praying with faith always, not wishing for an answer but simply wondering when the answer will come. God hears you. Pray in His will, and He will answer you. It may not be exactly the scenario you had in your head, but most of the time, it is so much more!

Lord Jesus,

I know you hear me and care about every aspect of my life. I want to be in your will, and I want my desires to be your desires. I am confident that you hear my prayer and know my heart. I will wait expectantly for your answer as I seek to honor you each day. Thank you for loving me and wanting to give me my heart's desires. I love you, Jesus. Amen.

Faith

"A mother's love is the fuel that enables a normal human being to do the impossible."
–Marion C. Garretty

We May Bend, but We Don't Break

"because you know that the testing of your faith produces perseverance."
James 1:3

O ur greatest moments of achievement and growth can be after some of our hardest trials. We don't realize how strong we are until we are pushed to the brink and our determination to persevere kicks in. Our daughter ran track and cross country in high school and had surgery on both knees with long recovery times. She would be in so much pain, and her legs would hurt as she was rebuilding strength and gaining her speed back. The coach would tell her it was okay to stop if she was hurting, but she pressed on. All athletes, to some degree, will push themselves to endure a little more each time to allow their bodies to become stronger, faster, and more equipped to perform.

I watched as she showed up to practice every day, even if it was to stretch or ride the stationary bike while she healed. I saw her slowly build back the muscle she had lost after surgery. I saw her run in the rain and on courses with obstacles and huge creeks to cross with her knee brace on. Sometimes, she would fall across the finish line, but she persevered. I saw her stumble, and I saw her get back up, and as her mom, I couldn't be prouder. We are going to have trials and obstacles that will try to defeat us and lead us away from our goal. Don't lose sight of your goal. Keep getting up even if you stumble.

In our spiritual lives, we all go through trials at some point that test our faith. Each time we endure a trial, we can choose to trust God instead of handling it on our own. Giving up control to allow God to work in a situation takes faith. When you add a little more faith to each trial you encounter, you are allowing yourself to persevere.

Have you ever noticed that when you are going through the hardest times, you reach out to God the most? If everything is smooth sailing, we aren't usually on our knees, pleading with God and praying constantly. It's in the toughest of times that we are tested and grow stronger. When the storm is over, we realize we withstood the worst and we survived. We persevered! If you read on to James 1:4, it says, "Let perseverance finish its work so that you may be mature and complete, not lacking anything." When we persevere, it helps us mature in our faith.

Loss, grief, heartache, defeat, anger, bitterness, pride, and despair will all test us beyond belief. We never realize how strong we are until we go through the hardest trials. When we realize that we may bend but don't break, we have learned what true perseverance is. Going through it can be challenging and overwhelming, but when you reach the other side, you can look back and see the person you have become and the inner strength you possess in Christ.

Moment to Reflect:

- ♥ Can you think about the trials you have had in your own life, and do you feel like you were stronger after you endured them?
- ♥ Do you feel like your faith would grow if it was never tested?
- ♥ Have you allowed God to refine you through trials, or has it made you resentful of the struggles?
- ♥ Have you ever had a nonbeliever watch how you handle a trial and ask you how you were able to get through it? It's a true testimony when we can rely on faith in times when we want to give up.

As I look back over my life so far, the times I remember my faith growing the most have been the moments when I have had to endure hard times. It's hard watching your child struggle and not being able to do much to help them. It's hard to want another child so much, but after a miscarriage and other testing, not knowing if you will be able to have one. It's hard to see your younger sibling suffering from a disease that takes the lives of so many and not being able to help her. We all have faced challenges, and I am no exception, but trials force you to your knees. They make you dig into Scripture like you never have before. They make you feel like you can't cry another tear or take another step, but somehow, you do. You do take another step, and you do cry out to God, and you do find that perfect verse that keeps you going and gives you hope because you are stronger than you think, and you can persevere!

Lord Jesus,

I don't know why I am going through this trial, but I need you to strengthen my faith. Help me to trust that you have this under control, and even though I am scared and feel like my world is crumbling, I will trust in you. Help me to find comfort in your word and strength in your still, small voice as you whisper words of comfort and hope to my soul. Thank you for bringing me through this and helping me become stronger even in my weakness. I love you, Jesus. Amen.

Invisible Doesn't Mean Impossible.

"Now faith is confidence in what we hope for and assurance about what we do not see."
Hebrews 11:1

Faith means putting all your hope into something that you can't visibly see. It's a lot easier to believe in something tangible that we can touch and feel. To put ourselves out there and believe in something invisible is difficult. But without faith, it would be hard to keep hope alive. Hope is what keeps us going when we face trials that shake us to our core. Hope keeps us positive when we want to give up. Hope helps us put one foot in front of the other and allows us to believe that tomorrow will be better.

Faith is like a generator that keeps your hope going when the power is out. You don't see it, but during the times you need it, it gives you the boost you need. Faith is believing in God's promises from the Bible. Faith is believing God will do something even when you can't see it. Many examples of faith from the Bible give us a clear picture of how faith can grow if you believe.

Moses went from doubting God could even use him because of a speech problem to leading over a million Israelites to the promised land. Noah built a boat that was over 450 feet long when there had never even been a drop of rain before. These men were ordinary, but their faith made them extraordinary. As a Christian mom, I want to live like that. I want to have faith so strong that if God spoke to my heart and wanted me to do something that seemed crazy, I would do it because of my faith in a God who wants the best for me. Look at what Noah would have missed if he hadn't built that boat. Moses would have missed meeting God on the mountain, holding the Ten Commandments, and parting the Red Sea. David had the faith to defeat a giant who was over 9 feet tall with only a slingshot. He knew God would help him win, even with no armor or protection from the giant.

How many times do we, as moms, feel we are not enough? We don't feel qualified, we aren't perfect, and we aren't like the other moms who seem to have everything together. God says He wants to use us because of our faults, not in spite of them. Our flaws make us human. Our faith is what makes us extraordinary.

Everyone in the Bible faced challenges, but they had the faith to overcome them with God's help. As moms, we will face challenges every single day with our kids and our families. God doesn't need the mom that has it all together. God needs the mom who is willing to step out of her comfort zone, armed with her slingshot, to lead the next generation of Christians toward the promised land. We're up against storms of every kind. We are facing giants in the form of movies, videos, suggestive lyrics, pornography, drugs, and much more. We can't fight these giants alone. We need faith in the God that can conquer the giants, calm the storm, heal the lame, deliver nations from famine and war, and raise the dead.

Moment to Reflect:

- ♥ Have you had a time in your life when you had to step out in faith and allow God to work?
- ♥ Why do you think God wants us to believe in something we can't see?
- ♥ Why does our faith grow more after trials?
- ♥ How can I let some of the heroes of the Bible inspire my faith to be stronger?

When I think about Noah, Moses, and David and all they had to endure, I think about how strong their faith must have been. They were asked to do things that were counter-cultural. Noah had to stand up to the crowd, Moses had to walk away from his old life, and David had to step into a role meant for an experienced warrior. They all had to take a chance, believing that God would step up and save them. It took extraordinary faith. It's no different than what He calls us to do today. Are you willing to stand up to giants who want to destroy your children? Are you willing to be available like Moses, even if you think you aren't qualified? Have faith; you can do it through Christ!

Lord Jesus,

When I read about some of the heroes in the Bible, I am in awe of their faith. The crazy thing is, they were ordinary people who just chose to have faith that you would do what you said you would do. I want to have faith like that. I want to be sure of what I hope for and certain of what I don't see. Increase my faith in you as I trust you more and more in my life. Amen.

Small but Strong

---

*"Because you have so little faith. Truly I tell you, if you
have faith as small as a mustard seed, you can say to this
mountain, 'Move from here to there' and it will move. Nothing
will be impossible for you."*
Matthew 17:20

D o you have a huge problem in your life that makes you doubt your strength and faith in God to handle it? He only needs a little faith, as small as a mustard seed. Show Him your small amount of faith, and He can move that mountain. If you look at Matthew 17:14, it gives a little background about our verse today from Matthew 17:20. Jesus came upon a crowd, and a man approached Him, kneeling with his son in his arms. He asked Jesus to have mercy, for his son was suffering greatly from seizures. The man had brought his son to the disciples, but they couldn't heal him. Jesus was frustrated by the unbelief of the disciples and asked the man to bring his son to him. Jesus rebuked the demon that was inside the boy, and he was healed. His disciples approached Jesus later and asked him why they had been unable to heal the boy. Jesus replied, "Because you have so little faith. I tell you the truth, if you have faith as small as a mustard seed, you can say to this mountain, 'Move from here to there,' and it will move. Nothing will be impossible for you."

Jesus told the disciples they lacked faith, and their unbelief stopped their ability to perform miracles. They didn't place their complete trust in Jesus. Jesus told them it only requires a little bit of true faith to make God want to move in someone's life. Your "mountain" could be a strong-willed child who has turned their back on God, or a rocky marriage, a health crisis, or a job loss. Whatever it is, have faith that God can move the "mountain."

Jesus used the mustard seed in his illustration because it is so tiny. Our faith may be very small, but what matters is what we place our faith in. Even a small amount of faith, when placed in Christ, can lead to extraordinary accomplishments through Him.

It's when we misplace our faith that we become like the disciples in this story, and we lose our impact. As Christians, so many of us try to handle things on our own, and we bear the burden ourselves instead of trusting in Jesus to share it. God showed my husband and me this truth when we were praying to have a second child. We placed our faith in ourselves and our doctors, resulting in disappointment and frustration. When we chose to put our small amount of faith in the mighty one who creates all things and makes the impossible possible, we were amazed at His goodness and grace. Jesus offers a better way by asking us to continually depend on Him in every situation. He can change circumstances. He can change hearts. He can heal. He can provide. What a blessing to know that even if we just have a tiny bit of faith, God can work with that!

Moment to Reflect:

♥ When you have a crisis in your life, do you try to handle it on your own?

♥ Can you think of some areas of your life where you need to have more faith? Can you evaluate those areas and ask God to grow your faith in those areas?

♥ Have you seen God move a mountain in your life, and if so, how did that grow your faith?

♥ God wants to use you to do incredible things. If you feel the Holy Spirit nudging you in a certain direction, pray about it and ask God for the faith to move that mountain.

Even the disciples who were chosen directly by Jesus had times when their faith was lacking. They may have gotten caught up in performing miracles and started relying on themselves more than God. We all do it to some extent. This is why it is so important to stay grounded in His Word, keeping our focus on Him and not ourselves. He needs us "all in" all the time.

Lord Jesus,

I know that if the disciples struggled with their faith sometimes, then I am bound to have times when I struggle too. Help me to be aware of when I try to handle things on my own and help me to reach for you. Increase my faith and help me to continually depend on you because I know you are strong enough to handle any situation. Help my prayer life to be consistent and help me to be aware of any areas of weakness in my faith so I can strengthen them. Just like the mustard seed grows when you water it, help me to water my faith by constantly seeking you, in your word, through bible study, and serving others. I want my faith to be strong. I love you, Jesus. Amen.

DAY 46

Power, Plain and Simple

---

*"so that your faith might not rest on human wisdom,
but on God's power."*
1 Corinthians 2:5

God has truly anointed Beth Moore and Lysa TerKeurst to speak His message. They are both Godly women who know the Bible and fear God. Every time I hear them or I am part of a study with them as the speaker, I am amazed at their knowledge and their ability to communicate God's message. But my faith should not be with them. I love to listen to Natalie Grant, Lauren Daigle, Nicole Nordeman, and Tasha Layton. Their music inspires me and helps me to be in a worshipful mood. But my faith is in the God they sing about, not them.

Our faith should not be in any person, speaker, preacher, gospel singer, or evangelist. Many speakers are well-versed in the Bible and present it eloquently, but it's not their presentation that should impress me. God's power should be what I place my faith in and what motivates me to believe.

As we teach our kids to have faith, we need to remember that although many of the speakers and singers today are incredibly talented, they are also human. We need to help our kids recognize the gospel truth without all the distractions of theatrics, lights, and sound. This allows them to hear the message God wants them to hear and see His power at work. God's power is what answers prayers. It heals the sick when we pray. It keeps loved ones safe in the storm. It restores marriages and friendships, helping the lost find forgiveness and grace.

If we place our faith in a doctor performing surgery on a loved one, we acknowledge the doctor's wisdom and skill. However, unless we also trust in God's power to work through that doctor, our prayers might not be as effective. The doctor is human and limited to what he or she can physically do, but with God's power, anything is possible.

We cannot see God's power, but we know it is there, and it is limitless. My goal is to be careful to put my faith in God's power and not in a person I may admire. If I place my faith in anything besides God's power, I will eventually be disappointed. This is a hard lesson for our kids to learn because so many of them have artists they like to listen to, athletes they like to watch play or actors they like to watch in movies. Even Christian athletes, singers, and actors mess up. We are all human, capable of making bad decisions or not following the right path. We need to point our kids to Christ and make sure they know He is the one with the power to move mountains.

God has done amazing things, and as I share with my kids and encourage them to share with others, I just try to speak from the heart. Sometimes, we might be in the car or be in a situation that is really very simple, but I can see a correlation with Christ and His love. I'll take that opportunity to share with my kids. Simple, down-to-earth conversation is the best way to point people towards Christ. I want them to trust in God's Word, not be bored by a long speech with words they can't pronounce. If they trust in God's Word, they will trust in His power, not ours. It's all about Him.

Moment to Reflect:

- ♥ Do you have a favorite speaker or Christian singer you like to listen to?
- ♥ Does your favorite speaker or singer point you to Christ or themselves?
- ♥ Are you guilty of trying to be too perfect when sharing the message of Christ?
- ♥ God just wants a humble heart willing to clearly speak the message of Christ so that others can see His power for themselves.

So often, we find ourselves striving for perfection when spreading the message of Christ. We elevate others and put them on a pedestal when they should be pointing others to Christ. Make sure your faith rests in God's power and not in the wisdom of man. It's easy to get distracted and swayed by grand productions. Jesus himself said in Luke 5: 31-32 that it is not the healthy who need a doctor, but the sick. If we are worried about looking perfect, we take away from pointing others to the need for a savior.

Lord Jesus,

Help me to be true in my faith to honor you and have faith in your power and not in the wisdom of men. Men's wisdom and men's power are limited, but your power is limitless. I pray that as I share the message of Christ, I will be clear and plainly present the gospel and point people to you and not myself. Strengthen my faith as I trust in your power in every area of my life. Amen.

Fireproof

"These have come so that your proven genuineness of your faith – of greater worth than gold, which perishes even though refined by fire – may result in praise, glory and honor when Jesus Christ is revealed."
1 Peter 1:7

My pastor often reminds our congregation that trials are inevitable. You can't go through life without going through trials. He often tells us, "You are usually in one of three places: about to go through a trial, right in the middle of a trial, or just coming out of a trial." When the verse says, "These have come," it is talking about trials in your life. It's never a question of if you will have them, only a question of when.

As I was studying 1 Peter 1:7 in my Study Bible, I came upon a story about pottery and how it relates to trials in our own lives. Back in Biblical times, the potters would bake clay pots to make them stronger. During the process, the intense heat would cause the pots with flaws to crack, but the ones that survived were marked as the Greek word "dokimos," which means "proven" or "genuine."

What a beautiful illustration for our own lives. The pots were baked for a short period of time, just like the temporary nature of our trials. They can be intense and test our beliefs and faith, just like the intense heat tested the pottery. We must ensure that our faith is strong enough to withstand the intensity of our trials so that we may be proven genuine, just like the pottery that survived the baking process.

The next part of verse 7 talks about our faith being of greater worth than gold, which perishes even though refined by fire. To place faith above gold says volumes about the value and importance of faith. Gold must also be put under intense heat to melt it and allow the impurities to come to the surface. After the goldsmith skims the impurities off the top, he determines how pure the gold is by seeing if he can see his reflection in it. When we are put through the fire and intense heat of trials, can others see the beauty of Christ in our reflection? This is genuine faith: the faith that reaches others in the name of Christ.

The next time you come across a clay pot or look down at the rings you may wear, ask yourself if your faith is strong enough to withstand the intense heat of the trials you may go through. Tell God you want to have a genuine faith that is tested, tried, and true.

Moment to Reflect:

♥ Have you been through trials in your life, and if so, how did you handle them?

♥ Is your faith strong enough to withstand an intense trial?

♥ How can you increase your faith so that when the trials come, you are prepared to withstand the heat?

♥ Do others see a reflection of Christ in you when you go through hard times?

I have often wondered, when I look at some families and see the trials they have gone through, how they were able to be so strong despite their circumstances. It is so easy to blame God and be angry when bad things happen, but those are the times when we need to be strongest. I want to be genuine, like the pot that withstood the fire and the gold that provided a reflection.

Lord Jesus,

I know trials are going to come. I want to have the faith to be able to withstand the heat no matter what comes my way. Help me to trust in you and become stronger through bad circumstances so others can see Christ in my reflection. Amen.

Are You Using Your Gift?

> *"I long to see you so that I may impart to you some spiritual gift to make you strong - that is, that you and I may be mutually encouraged by each other's faith."*
> *Romans 1:11-12*

Did you know that when you become a Christian, you receive a spiritual gift unique to you? We all have different gifts, so we can help others in different ways. If you know someone who likes to plan, organize, and supervise others, they might have the spiritual gift of administration. This gift can be used in multiple ways, from steering leaders in the right direction to a volunteer position as director of Vacation Bible School. You can use your gift in your career, in a volunteer position, at your child's school, or in your community.

Other examples of spiritual gifts are discernment, encouragement, evangelism, faith, giving, hospitality, leadership, mercy, service, and teaching. Each of these gifts helps to make up the body of Christ. Knowing what area we are gifted in helps us to know which ministries to plug into and where to focus our time. We can also encourage our children to recognize their spiritual gifts when they are saved! It's a great way to let them be involved in areas that interest them as they minister to others. You are never too young to use your gifts and abilities to serve God.

Knowing your spiritual gifts can strengthen you and make you more effective as a Christian. The gift of hospitality can help someone feel welcome in your home and show them the love of Jesus. The gift of mercy can show kindness and compassion to those who others may cast aside or ignore. Those who have experienced mercy may be more open to hearing the gospel simply because someone showed they cared. The gift of teaching is a true treasure because you can impart lessons to others and help them understand something that was confusing to them before. The gift of faith is very important for missionaries who put their lives on the line every day in hostile countries. They rely on God to get them through and show others the importance of trusting in God when things seem impossible.

Can you see how using our spiritual gifts can help benefit others? We can all encourage someone else by using the gifts God gave us to build up the body of Christ.

Moment to Reflect:

- ♥ Have you surrendered your whole heart and life to Jesus as your Lord and Savior? If so, do you know what your spiritual gifts are? If you are not yet a Christian, I would love for you to continue reading this devotional because you are on the right track to learning more about God and growing in your knowledge of Him. If you have questions about becoming a Christian, please see my section at the end of the book, which walks you through this process.

- ♥ What are the best ways for you to know what your spiritual gift(s) are? You can always start by getting involved in several ministry opportunities. Find ministries that interest you and ones where you feel you are the most useful. Often, people will compliment and affirm your abilities in a certain area, and this will let you know you are heading in the right direction.

- ♥ You can also find free tests online and answer a series of multiple-choice questions that will automatically tell you what your top spiritual gifts are. One website is www.giftstest.com. It asks for your name and email so it can send you your results, and it only takes five minutes to complete the test.

- ♥ Have you been in a situation where you saw another person's spiritual gift in action and how it benefited others?

- ♥ How has your faith grown by someone else using their spiritual gifts to help you?

I never knew there were so many spiritual gifts and what a difference they can make in other's lives! There are so many ways, not only in careers but even volunteering, where I can use my spiritual gifts to show others the love of Christ. I can see what Paul meant when he wrote that we could be mutually encouraged by each other's faith as we use our unique spiritual gifts to help others.

Lord Jesus,

I know I am a child of yours, and I ask that you show me areas where you can use me and the gifts you have given me to draw others to you. I am uniquely qualified to step out in faith and utilize my spiritual gifts to teach, encourage, lead, have mercy, serve, and be hospitable to others. Help others grow in faith because I chose to use the gifts you have given me to glorify you. I love you, Jesus. Amen.

Example

"So many times, you will feel like you've failed, but in the eyes,
heart, and mind of your child, you are supermom."
–Stephanie Precourt

It's Not About You

"Be completely humble and gentle; be patient, bearing with one another in love."
Ephesians 4:2

---

have a confession to make. I used to chew two or three pieces of bubble gum at my son's baseball games so my mouth would be too full of gum to say anything sarcastic or rude to the umpire if I lost my temper. I know that doesn't sound very Christian of me, but I am incredibly competitive, and I got into the games. I was vocal enough for my girls to notice and ask me if I brought my gum with me to be sure my mouth was occupied during the game. This verse in Ephesians would have been a great one to remember as I was tempted to shout at the umpire. Have you ever had a situation when maybe another player pushed, tackled, or shoved your child in an unsportsmanlike manner that made you want to retaliate? I'm sure you have been cut off in traffic or pushed out of your position in line because someone was in a hurry. We have all had flights delayed or maybe worked with someone at a job or on a committee who didn't pull their weight. When someone wrongs us, we want to hold onto the hurt and blame rather than let it go and forgive. It's important to remember that Christ forgave us when He didn't have to.

If you have been in these situations, or any like them, you know how hard it is to be patient, much less humble and gentle. I have been at a restaurant when the waiter got my order wrong multiple times. When you are hungry and have had to wait a long time for your meal, it can be frustrating when someone else's mistake affects you, too. These are all situations where this verse could help us strive to be a better example to our kids and others who may be watching. When Paul says in Ephesians to bear with one another in love, it means that everyone struggles and has burdens that can affect their performance and how they serve. By shifting focus from myself and considering others' perspectives and circumstances, it becomes easier to share their burden.

It is hard to be kind and compassionate if we are being self-centered. We must be able to take the focus off ourselves and think of others. The shallower we are, the more we will be irritated when someone interrupts our plans or makes a mistake. I don't want to miss a chance to lead someone to Christ because of my selfishness and lack of self-control.

We have all found ourselves in these types of situations at sports events, work, or the store. When someone acts out of humility and gives a gentle answer, it provides peace to the entire situation since it's hard to have a conflict with someone being nice. It takes a great deal of self-control to be humble and gentle when we want to scream, shout, and lose our temper. There are so many times when I have had an opportunity to respond with patience and love, and I didn't. The lasting effects on those observing can be life-changing. Jesus tells us in Matthew 22: 36-39 that the greatest commandment is to love Him with all of our heart and soul. The second commandment is to love your neighbor. It's hard to do the second without the first.

We show the love of Christ when we answer in a gentle tone and have patience. I still remember when my oldest daughter was about a year and a half old, and we had monitors in the room to hear her at night or naptime. One day, our monitor picked up interference from our neighbor across the street who had a daughter who was about four. The little girl had done something to get in trouble, and she was in time-out. The mom came to talk to her, and I remember how gentle and soothing her voice was. I wasn't trying to listen, but I was amazed at how she handled the situation! She never raised her voice, asking her daughter if she knew why she was in trouble. The daughter answered, and the mom explained why her actions were being punished. She then did something I will never forget: she prayed with her daughter. Every word from her mouth was kind, compassionate, and humble. With her gentle amen, she had me in tears! Her example made me want to be more like that with my own child. I wanted to incorporate gentleness and kindness instead of harshness or impatience.

That mom has no idea how much she touched another mother's life forever that day. You never know as well when a gentle answer or a kind comment can bring someone closer to Christ. If we can let Christ be our example in humility, gentleness, patience, kindness, compassion, and forgiveness, we will reflect Christ's love on anyone we encounter.

Moment to Reflect:

♥ Can you relate to any of the examples of ways that test our humility, gentleness, and patience?

♥ Have you responded in a way that showed kindness and compassion, and if so, how did it change the situation or make a difference?

♥ Has there been a situation when you responded with forgiveness and compassion that led to you being able to share the gospel?

♥ Will you commit today's verse to memory so that when stressful situations occur in your life, God will bring it to your mind for you to respond in the right way?

Committing this verse to memory will help us focus on what we need to do in hectic situations that call for kindness and compassion. I pray we will respond appropriately.

Lord Jesus,

I am human, and sometimes, when I get stressed, I don't act in humility and gentleness. Help me to take the focus off myself and realize that others are going through trials, too, and I need to be more understanding when I don't know the whole story. I pray for kindness and compassion to flow from me so that people seeing how I react are not turned away from Jesus. I pray I will never let bitterness overtake me and that I will learn to forgive and give others a chance just as Christ gave me one. Thank you for this verse, Lord, and help me to hide it in my heart so you can speak it to me in times of trouble. I love you, Jesus. Amen.

The Best Things Come in Small Packages

"Don't let anyone look down on you because you are young, but set an example for the believers in speech, in conduct, in love, in faith, and in purity."
1 Timothy 4:12

Teaching our children 1 Timothy 4:12 is crucial. Adults are not the only ones with influence, and many times, adults can learn so much from the example of a young person. I have witnessed high schoolers get up early and meet middle schoolers at 6:30 a.m. on a school morning to lead a bible study and pray with them before school. They have no idea what influence they have on the other kids. Friends are often more receptive to peers than adults, providing young people a powerful chance to set an example through their words, conduct, love, faith, and purity.

I have three children, and the influence that I have seen each of them have on others' lives is incredible. They have no idea the other friends or younger ones coming along behind them who are watching their every move. I remember when my kids were little, we painted their playroom. I chose a wall that they would see each time they entered the playroom, and I painted this verse from 1 Timothy 4:12 on it. I wanted Scripture to be ingrained in them so that when they encountered others who made them feel insignificant or unimportant, they would know the truth. We have participated in family mission trips where I watched them engage with children from diverse backgrounds. They played games, assisted with crafts, taught Bible stories, and organized sports activities. I have witnessed how they treated the foster kids we were hosting in our home like they were part of our family. I have also worked alongside them in VBS and observed them leading small Bible studies as mentors for younger kids. When Christ is involved, age doesn't matter.

God likes to use the people you would least expect, and young people are invaluable in His kingdom for reaching others for Christ. As moms, we have an obligation and a mission to empower our children with Scripture and pray over them daily to strengthen their faith. They are the future of this world, and we are their cheerleaders who can help them know how important they are to Christ.

What our children listen to makes a difference. What they watch stays with them. Make sure they know that their choices in music, shows, and movies may impact their witness for Christ. How they speak when we aren't around sets an example, whether good or bad, to those around them. Their integrity is so important. How they act when we aren't with them demonstrates their character. Whether they realize it or not, others are watching and looking up to them, and they have an opportunity to set a good example. They can lead prayers on their sports team or have Bible studies with their dance or cheer team. God placed them in their groups and positions for a reason.

As moms, make sure your children know the message of 1 Timothy 4:12 and how important they are in God's kingdom.

Share with them how they encourage you in your faith by seeing them make a difference in others' lives. God uses the least of us to do powerful things. Pray over your children, pray with your children, and let them know their importance in setting an example for believers everywhere.

Moment to Reflect:

- ♥ Does your child know what a difference they can make in God's Kingdom and how important they are even though they are young?
- ♥ Do you talk to your kids about what they listen to, what they watch, and why it is important not to corrupt your mind with the things of this world?
- ♥ Do your kids know how important integrity is, and that how they choose to act when you aren't around shows their true character and can affect their witness for Christ?
- ♥ Will you pray 1 Timothy 4:12 over your child and even write it on an index card and put it in a prominent place in your home so they will see it regularly?

When your children realize that no matter how young they are, they can make a difference for Christ, it will affect their lives. Help your kids live out this verse, whether they are toddlers or teens. Encourage them in their walk with Christ so they can be leaders at school, the ball field, dance practice, or wherever they go. They could be the only representation of Jesus someone may ever see.

Lord Jesus,

As a mom, I have a huge opportunity to train my kids to love you and follow you. No matter how young they are, they can be used by you to reach others for Christ. I ask that you help me encourage them to learn this verse and live their lives as an example to others. May their words, actions, love for others, and purity serve as an example, showing others that they can live this way as well. Guide me in constantly praying for Your blessings to be upon them as they grow to become more like You. Amen.

The Lost Need Your Love

"Do to others as you would have them do to you."
Luke 6:31

Without God's help, it is almost impossible to live out Luke 6:31. The human side desires to retaliate against those who have been malicious or cruel towards us. Treating someone who has wronged us with respect and kindness takes a whole new level of sanctification. We can't expect our children to treat others the way they want to be treated if we don't model this for them. Luke 6:31 directs us as believers to love our enemies, show goodness to those who hate us, and give blessings to those who curse us. That is asking a lot, but our kids are watching our example!

Jesus doesn't want us to retaliate when someone wrongs us. So, when we are mistreated and feel used, are we supposed to pray for the person who has wronged us? Sometimes, it feels impossible. It may take every bit of strength we have to pray for someone we dislike. I have even been humbled by one of my children, who reminded me to show love even when I don't want to. Our kids are listening and watching us more than we realize.

There's no way I could do this on my own. The love we should show to those who are unkind to us can only come from our Heavenly Father. I've had people in the past mistreat someone I cared about, and although I wanted to hate them, I knew it was important to show love because God wanted me to. When we show this kind of love, the wrongful person sees Jesus through us. They expect hate, but when we show love instead, it can open a door for them to see God's mercy and grace. It's amazing how showing grace to someone who doesn't deserve it can soften our own hearts and take the bitterness away.

It might take time, but it's difficult to hold negative feelings or act unkindly towards someone when you're praying for them daily and consistently making an effort to show them kindness. It isn't something that comes naturally, so we need to be walking in truth and fellowship with God to be able to hear His Spirit telling us to love and pray. Simply by doing unto others as we would have them do to us can show them the love of Jesus in a way that a sermon never could. They aren't expecting us to show love when they wrong us. It gets their attention and points them to Jesus!

In this crazy world, there is a lack of compassion when a need arises and a sense of spitefulness and hostility when we should be showing love. We have shut God out of so much that this world needs believers to step up and show the lost a little grace. The way we respond to a situation and how we choose to treat someone, regardless of how they treat us, could be the difference between heaven and hell for someone else.

You never know how just a kind word or a compassionate response can make a difference in the life of someone who is lost. As you run across situations that make you angry or want to retaliate, take a deep breath and show love instead. Unless the lost hear the gospel through our words and actions and believe in the grace that none of us deserve, they are destined for eternity in hell. When I think about the lasting effects of retaliation and the influence I could have for good, treating others the way I would like to be treated doesn't seem so hard! We are all broken and in need of mercy and grace. I know I require a huge amount of grace, and Jesus gives it to me even though I did nothing to earn it. I need to extend that same grace to others.

Moment to Reflect:

- ♥ Do you have someone in your life who is difficult to like? How can Luke 6:31 help you develop a better attitude toward them?
- ♥ When you encounter situations in public that make you want to retaliate, will you live out Luke 6:31 instead?
- ♥ Will you make a list of people who have wronged you in the past and pray for them?
- ♥ Are there lost people in your realm of influence? Can you list ways you can show love and compassion to them to make a difference for eternity?

Extending compassion and love to someone who has wronged you is one of the hardest things God asks us to do. We would rather think of all the ways we could get back at them, but that is not what God wants us to do. He wants us to love them and treat them with kindness so that if they are lost, they will see the love of Jesus pouring out of us. It could make a difference for their eternity.

Lord Jesus,

I don't always have nice thoughts when it comes to certain people in my life. I pray that you would help me to have a heart of compassion and love toward those who have wronged me or who are rude and hateful to me or my loved ones. Treating others the way I want to be treated is a measure of grace, and I need every ounce of strength you can provide to make it happen. I want to show the love of Jesus to those who don't know you. Let them see you through my actions, and let my actions make them want you in their life. I love you, Jesus! Amen.

Being the Light Helps Others See Through the Darkness

"In everything set them an example by doing what is good. In your teaching show integrity, seriousness, and soundness of speech that cannot be condemned, so that those who oppose you may be ashamed because they have nothing bad to say about us."
Titus 2:7-8

Oh, how I wish that those who oppose me had nothing bad to say about me! I think of myself as a good mom, but I know that I get impatient in the car and may use the words "idiot" or "stupid" as I am driving in traffic. I believe the phrases "Are you kidding me?" and "Seriously?" have also graced my lips. When you have little ones, even tweens and soon-to-be drivers, riding in the car with you, you need to set a good example for listening ears. I am preaching to myself on this one.

Titus 2: 7-8 doesn't say, "Set a good example when you are riding in the car." It says, "In everything." I need to be living with integrity in everything I do so that when those who may not like me try to find something bad about me, they can't! This verse doesn't say I have to be perfect. I just have to make good choices in how I live and in what I say. My integrity means everything to my witness as a mom and as a Christian. I want my kids to know I am honest and that I live a life that is uncompromising in my morals and values. If I'm trying to teach them to live with integrity and love Jesus, I need to show that's how I live as well. As my kids observe this example, so do others who are watching. We never know what a difference we can make in someone else's life just by the choices we make on our own.

Remember this: Doing good goes beyond simply making good choices. It's also doing the right thing, even when you stand alone. As a parent, making decisions about your kids can often feel isolating. Sometimes, it seems like all the other parents let their kids have free reign, and you are the only one standing your ground. My husband and I have noticed this pattern with various friends of our kids. The rules for cell phones, curfews, dating, parties, clothing attire, and many more issues have been the complete opposite of the rules we set in place for our kids. We stood firm in following what we believed God was guiding us to do for them and did not give in, even though other parents were more lenient. Hang in there. Your kids will see you had their best interest at heart one day.

Integrity is key to being a positive example, as it involves making the right decisions even when no one else is around. By maintaining our integrity in challenging times and staying honest even when others succeed through cheating and deceit, we set an example that allows others to see Christ reflected in us. Actions often speak louder than words.

The world often looks for our mistakes to criticize us as Christians. While we are imperfect and will make errors, we should strive to live with integrity and set a positive example. This way, when people oppose us, they won't have anything negative to say. When we find ourselves surrounded by bad influences, immorality, and violence, we should remember that Jesus is the light that overcame darkness. By living with integrity, His light can shine through us as well.

Moment to Reflect:

- ♥ Do you realize others are paying attention to how you act and what you do, and your example matters for Christ?
- ♥ Are there ways you can strive to live with more integrity as you seek to honor God through your example?
- ♥ If others called you out right now, would they be able to say anything negative about you concerning your speech or actions outside of church?
- ♥ Commit Titus 2:7-8 to memory and strive to bring it to mind when confronted with choices that could test your integrity. Choose wisely.

Setting a good example in everything we do can be exhausting. We are human. We are not perfect. We make mistakes. Ask God to lead and guide you to turn away from areas that could bring your integrity into question. Let your words and your actions reflect the love of Christ.

Lord Jesus,

I want my life to be a great example of your love in this dark world. I pray that I will live a life of integrity and be intentional about my actions and my words. I pray for your strength to guide me in the decisions I make so I will teach my children integrity and others will not be able to find anything bad about me. I want my light to shine for you in everything I do. Amen.

Don't Hide Your Light

"In the same way, let your light shine before others, that they may see your good deeds and glorify your Father in heaven."
Matthew 5:16 ESV

What is the first thing you do if you walk into a dark room and can't see anything? Probably turn on a light or a lamp. A lamp is placed on a table or a stand to give it enough height to shine into more space. As Christians, we are the light that is meant to shine and reach people in this dark world. How can we do that?

We can provide the light that those in darkness are searching for. I think of myself more like a nightlight. We have them all over our house. We even take them on vacations with us so when it's dark, we can see in unfamiliar areas. Nightlights are always there, but they shine only when the darkness comes. They show you where you need to step and light the path for safety. As Christians, we should always be available when someone needs us, willing to shine our light so others see the path to Christ.

We, as mothers, possess the power to shape our children's lives. Let's lead the way for them. If they are younger, give them a big hug, listen to them, and care about what matters to them.

Have devotions with them, pray with them, and use everyday events to teach them about Jesus. If they are teens or older, they still need that hug! They still need you to pray for them. They may not talk but give them encouragement anyway. We all need encouragement, no matter who we are or how old we are. Smile at the neighbor passing by, the dry cleaner, the cashier at the store, or even a stranger. Text your husband or a friend to let them know how important they are in your life. You can also offer hope to someone experiencing tremendous heartbreak and pain. Just a little bit of encouragement can go such a long way for someone who is struggling.

One thing that is hard for me but invaluable to reaching others is patience. I sincerely struggle with that one! Whether you are dealing with a child, a loved one who is healing or sick, a lost neighbor who is alone and needs your care, or a stranger who is having a bad day, patience can speak volumes to someone who needs the love of Christ.

This world is broken. The lost need hope. There is despair without peace, chaos without contentment, and sorrow without joy. The Holy Spirit inside us lights the flame, but it is our job to carry that light into the dark world and shine it for others to see Christ. We can't hide our light, because if we do, others might not see Jesus. Even a tiny sliver of light in a dark and desolate place brings hope to the hopeless. How we treat others and conduct ourselves reveals to the lost a light that reflects Christ. By responding with patience or kindness instead of sternness, sarcasm, or meanness, we display Christ within us, giving Him the glory for our actions.

When we smile, help a stranger, hug someone who is broken, call someone who is lonely, or take a meal to someone sick, we are shining our light into the darkness. Don't ever underestimate what your light can do for God's kingdom. Even one star in the vast sky can be seen clearly in the dark. Imagine what all our lights could do if we choose to shine for Jesus every day!

Moment to Reflect:

- ♥ Have you been in a situation where everyone around you was scared or angry, and you were able to offer hope or an encouraging word?
- ♥ Has someone else changed your day or even your life by shining their light in your darkness?
- ♥ Do you need to make some changes in how you do things so your light will be able to reach others for Christ?
- ♥ Can you commit to memorizing Matthew 5:16 so that when a situation arises, you won't hide your light if others need to see it?

We underestimate the significant impact our reactions and responses can have on others, whether it's in the workplace, with our children, or among other parents. A kind word, a smile, a meal, or simply spending time with someone can make a huge difference to someone who is hurting.

A patient reaction when someone is expecting anger gives hope that maybe this world is not completely in the dark. Help others to see the way to Christ by shining your light.

Lord Jesus,

I may not think that what I do matters, but you put your Holy Spirit inside of me, and I need to let it shine. Help me as I encounter problems or issues to handle them with a gentle heart and a kind word. Help me to have compassion for others and what they may be going through. I pray I will never be too busy to lend a hand to someone who needs it. Thank you for giving us hope, even in a dark world. Help me shine for you! Amen.

You Serve a Greater Purpose

"Whatever you do, work at it with all your heart, as working for the Lord, not for men."
Colossians 3:23

Whether you are a stay-at-home mom, work-from-home mom, or work outside the home mom, I think we can safely say we all have a job to do. God considered work as a gift to enjoy, which is why he gave Adam a job right after He created him. Adam and Eve were in charge of all the creatures on the ground, the birds in the sky, and the fish in the sea. And I thought I had a handful with my three kids! No matter what you define as work, we should embrace it as a blessing and express gratitude for it. Sometimes, the tasks we must do may seem tedious or even trivial, but they serve a purpose. We serve a God who gave us our gifts and abilities for a reason. When you feel stuck in the routine of daily life or overwhelmed by constant pressure, it's normal to question the significance of what you're doing. However, it's important to understand that your current situation has a purpose. Everything you're going through is part of a larger plan, even if it's not immediately clear. Embrace the idea that there is meaning in your circumstances, as they fit into a bigger picture that may not be obvious right now.

He has allowed you to positively influence those you serve. You may have co-workers, or you may be in charge of the next generation for Christ. Either way, you are part of a labor of love. We should put forth our best effort with a good attitude and respect for all authority. We should be willing to take on the responsibilities and tasks we are assigned with a cheerful heart. When we do this, we bring honor to Christ.

If we are tasked with a job and fail to give our best effort, it can impact our testimony. This includes motherhood. When my husband and I signed up to do foster care, we had to take multiple classes, attend several meetings, read manuals, watch videos, take tests, and get references to become foster parents. I remember reading the letters of reference we asked for from neighbors, friends, and staff members at our church. The reference letters were heartwarming as others expressed that we were good parents and that other children would be blessed to be in our home. It made me realize how important it is to always do your best at whatever God has called you to do. People are watching, and your witness for Christ is at stake.

Full-time moms often dedicate countless hours to caring for their families, managing household tasks, and providing emotional support. Despite the tireless effort they put in, their hard work can often go unnoticed and unappreciated. Much of the work you do happens without fanfare, often behind the scenes. Your kids don't typically express appreciation by saying, "Good job," nor do they reward your efforts with a raise or promotion. You are expected to feed, nurture, doctor, referee, teach, train, chauffeur, and counsel, all while disciplining, keeping them safe, and pointing them to Christ. It is one of the hardest jobs we could accept, but also the most rewarding. Just because we work behind the scenes, we still need to give it our best. Our children rely on us, and if we become lax in discipline or teaching them right from wrong, we are failing them.

We are raising the next generation for Christ, and we can shape this world for the better when we set a good example for them! In any role we undertake, it is important to recognize that our actions and behaviors are being closely observed by others. This includes how we approach different situations, the way we carry out our responsibilities, and the level of integrity we exhibit in all aspects of our work. When we show up late, leave early, cut corners, or act dishonestly, we are not doing a good job of showing Christ to nonbelievers.

This can be extremely difficult if you have a job where you feel unappreciated. It's frustrating – and humbling – to work for someone who doesn't respect you or makes you feel like you aren't doing anything right. Keep telling yourself that you are working for Christ, not for that person. Use the opportunity to show unbelievers that integrity matters in all situations. Don't ever lose hope in doing right.

Moment to Reflect:

- ♥ Have you been in a work situation where you felt unappreciated in everything you did? How did you handle it?
- ♥ Can you think of any improvements you can make in your job to set a better example for nonbelievers?
- ♥ Have you ever hired someone who cut corners or didn't give you their best? How did it affect your view of them or their chance of getting hired again in the future?
- ♥ Whether you are a stay-at-home mom or work outside the home, you have a job that requires your very best. Are you working for the Lord or for men?

It's easy to slack off and give yourself a break when the boss is away or when no one is looking. No matter how much we want to take it easy when we are working, we have a responsibility to our Heavenly Father to do our best so we don't ruin our witness for Him. The way we conduct ourselves in our jobs can affect the way nonbelievers view us. Remember as you go about your job that you aren't in it to please others but to please God. Always give your best, and God will be pleased.

Lord Jesus,

It's so hard to give 100% all the time. Help me to remember that when I get frustrated in a work situation, I need to trust that you can help me through it and I am working to glorify you, not my boss. I pray for patience when I am tested and endurance when I am weak. I pray for humbleness instead of pride and for the courage to do the right thing even if others aren't. You are my boss, Jesus, and my reward is in heaven. Amen.

DAY 55

Set Apart

"Finally, brothers and sisters, whatever is true, whatever is noble, whatever is right, whatever is pure, whatever is lovely, whatever is admirable – if anything is excellent or praiseworthy- think about such things."
Philippians 4:8

My kids used to get so annoyed when we all sat down in the den to watch a movie, only to end up turning it off after five minutes. The language in some movies, even years ago, was not what I thought was appropriate for my kids – or my husband and me! They didn't understand that when you allow filth to enter your mind, ears, and vision, it starts to seep in. Then, slowly, you start to allow more and more until, eventually, you have no standards by which to live.

The human mind is fascinating. The human mind is truly remarkable. God designed it to absorb vast amounts of information, think independently, and make decisions, but it is essential to have a filter. We can't listen, watch, and absorb things that are untrue, immoral, corrupt, or impure and expect not to have lasting repercussions from them. There are certain shows with ratings that we refuse to watch no matter what. We also have an app that allows us to filter movies and shows, taking out words we don't want to hear and scenes we don't feel are appropriate. This app allows us to still be in this world, experiencing comedy and adventures, but not be of this world with all the added curse words and scenes that go against our morals and values.

If we focus our minds on things that are true, noble, right, pure, and admirable, then it is much harder for Satan to get a foothold in our lives. Our thoughts can control our actions, so if we keep them pure, our actions should reflect a Christlike faith and example. When we act in humility, having grace and mercy, and showing compassion toward others, we are reflecting Christ. We can protect our thoughts in what we watch and hear, but we also need to guard against pride and other thought patterns that don't represent Christ. What we fill ourselves with is what comes out, so we must pursue Christ above all else.

If we don't allow impure thoughts, then we don't allow songs with inappropriate lyrics or shows and movies with inappropriate scenes. Facing the challenges of this world can be overwhelming, as it often feels like we are constantly battling against everyone just to do what is right. If your kids are still riding with you, then you have control of what they listen to in the car. As they grow, don't waste opportunities to encourage Christian music or explain why certain lyrics are inappropriate. As Christians, sometimes we have to make a hard call. It becomes even more challenging when your kids start driving, as you're not always there to monitor what they're listening to or the lyrics that may influence them. This is why training them from a young age to honor God and seek Him is so important.

If we truly want to make a difference for Christ, we must be set apart. If you find yourself caught in a moral gray area and entertaining questionable thoughts, it's not too late to seek God's guidance to choose the right path. Claim Philippians

4:8 in your life. Focus on pure, admirable things, and you will be able to serve Christ better and be more fruitful for Him.

Moment to Reflect:

♥ Have you allowed yourself to let down your guard with movies, shows, and songs that bring foul language and unbiblical scenes into your mind?

♥ Can you start trying to make a conscious effort to let your thoughts think about all the characteristics in this verse and see how it changes your views?

♥ Are there some changes you need to make in what you listen to or watch to be able to keep your mind focused on pure and admirable thoughts?

♥ Are you willing to be strong as a parent and make sure you are teaching your kids to think about these things and apply them to what they listen to and watch?

I know it's challenging to find a movie or show without offensive content these days. My husband and I have had to quit watching multiple shows that we really enjoyed because of the new characters or scenes producers are adding to appease the world. Without the app we have that filters, we wouldn't be able to watch much at all! Don't ever feel bad for doing the right thing. Keep your mind focused on things that are pure, right, and noble, and your actions will follow.

Lord Jesus,

It is so hard today to keep my thoughts focused on Godly things. Help me to focus on things that are pure, right, and admirable so that the things I listen to and watch will be acceptable to you. I pray that the example I set will show my children that I want to put you first and honor you with my thoughts and my actions. I love you, Jesus. Amen.

Friendship

"There is no way to be a perfect mother, but a million
ways to be a good one."
Jill Churchill

Ironmen Are Heroes for Christ

"As iron sharpens iron, so one man sharpens another."
Proverbs 27:17 BSB

Have you ever received a compliment that felt more like an insult? I have. Once, when I was in the youth group at my church, our youth minister had us all take turns sitting in a chair at the front, and everyone in the youth group had a chance to say something to the person in the hot seat. When it was my turn, there were some kind words spoken, but then one person said something I will never forget: "I admire Amy because she is consistent." I smiled, but on the inside, I was thinking, "What kind of compliment is that? Consistent? Who cares?" Later, my youth minister pulled me aside because he could see that I didn't think much of the comment. He said, "Amy, do you know how rare it is to find a teenager who is consistent in their walk with Christ? One who never wavers in their faith? You are someone that people can rely on to do the right thing and have integrity in their decisions. That is not just a compliment but one of the highest honors you could receive! There are people you don't even realize who look up to you because of your consistent faith. That strength of character helps sharpen others who are looking to you as their example." Well, when you put it like that, I guess consistency isn't so bad.

Have you thought about consistency in your parenting and how that stability is a great way to show our kids that our faith is unwavering? We can sharpen our children, our friends, and our family by allowing our positive mindset and actions of integrity to rub off on them and strengthen their faith and hope in Christ. Just like when two pieces of iron are rubbed against each other, each piece sharpens the other one. When we are in a close relationship with Christ, we can help and support others in their spiritual journey. Putting God first in everything we do not only benefits us but also sets a positive example for others, inspiring and encouraging them to better themselves. Making a choice to be in church on Sunday or be involved in other activities at church can show our kids and our friends that God is a priority to us.

You can help your kids notice God in action by taking the chance to discuss learning moments with them when a situation comes up. Sometimes, a friend or family member's circumstances allow for conversation about a certain topic or subject matter. You might come across news or TV reports about a troubled or suffering celebrity, and it can be a great conversation starter to discuss choices, priorities, and values and their significance. Don't ever waste a moment when you can sharpen your child's faith using real-life issues.

We can sharpen each other by strengthening our own relationship with Christ so we can be strong enough to encourage others. As we spend time with Christ, have our daily devotions and prayer time, and listen to what God has to say to us, we sharpen our faith to build up others. As we make good choices in what we listen to, watch, and say, we set an example for fellow friends who may need to change their priorities or choices to center around God. True friends are honest with each other and build each other up. At times, it is necessary to show tough love when a friend has lost their way and needs to be guided back onto the right path.

There are many ways we can help sharpen one another. Some days, you may be the one doing the sharpening, but other days, you may need to be the one who needs to be sharpened. Having a strong circle of Christian friends and being involved in a small group at church is essential for staying grounded in Christ and being held accountable. We all need encouragement, and sometimes, we need redirection when we go off course.

Make sure you are staying close to Christ and strengthening your faith so that when an opportunity arises, you are able to help sharpen someone else!

Moment to Reflect:

- ♥ Do you have someone in your life who helps to sharpen your faith in Christ? If so, let them know you appreciate them. Encouragement helps sharpen fellow Christians.
- ♥ What are some ways you can change your priorities to be able to sharpen your child's faith?
- ♥ Are you surrounding yourself with fellow believers and spending time with Christ and in His Word to sharpen your own faith?
- ♥ Ask God to reveal to you if there is a friend who needs sharpening. The Holy Spirit will nudge you in the direction you need to take to help that friend.

I love how the Bible uses so many metaphors to illustrate what we must do as Christians. God uses real situations and objects to teach us a lesson. Iron sharpening iron is a beautiful illustration of how we can picture ourselves as one piece, ready to sharpen a fellow believer through strength, faith, encouragement, and love.

Lord Jesus,

Help me to put you first in everything I do so that when the time comes, I will be able to help sharpen my children's faith and their walk with you. You give us so many ways to stay strong through prayer, faith, fellowship with other believers, and reading your word. I pray that I will strive to keep myself ready and available to meet my kids' needs and those of others when they need to be sharpened. Thank you, Lord, for allowing us to help fellow believers. Amen.

Priceless Treasures

"A friend loves at all times, and a brother is born for adversity."
Proverbs 17:17 BSB

I don't think God meant for us to live without friendship. Looking back on my life, I've found that the moments when I felt the happiest and most fulfilled were those when I was surrounded by friends who genuinely cared about me and took an interest in my life. I have found that some friendships last a lifetime, while others may only last a season. There are new friends God brings into our lives at a time when we need them the most, and it is exciting to me to think that God could have a new friend waiting for me just around the corner. Friends are special because they know the real you and have your own best interest at heart. They love you for you, and you can rely on them and trust them with your secrets. They ensure you stay on the right path and aren't afraid to guide you back and advise you to change your course if your choices are leading you astray.

Friendships are so important in motherhood – raising kids is hard, and it helps to have fellow moms to go through life with! Mom friends understand the worry that comes along with raising kids. They can also sense when you are stressed and in need of a break. They can share strategies they've used to organize, save time, or help with any issues your child may have. On days when I felt like the worst mom, a mom friend would often call and cheer me up, encouraging me to keep going. Having Christian friends by your side keeps you grounded as you raise the next generation through tantrums, scrapes, groundings, and heartaches. Surrounding yourself with a group of believers who build each other up and point their kids to Christ is the reason God created friendships.

Have you ever had a friend who initially seemed to be happy for you, but the more you were around them, the more they seemed to be jealous or envious? That is not a true friend. True friendship does not envy, and it also isn't rude or easily angered (1 Corinthians 13). True friends don't keep records of wrongs and throw them back at you when you have a disagreement. True friends want the best for you, and they are there to protect you and be patient with you when you are going through a rough time. Just as Proverbs 17:17 says, "A friend loves at all times." No matter what you are going through, they are there to comfort you. You may be going through a season of loneliness and need to know someone cares, or you may have dozens of friends in your life. Regardless of your circumstances, Jesus will always be your most steadfast friend, and you can always rely on Him for companionship.

The second part of the verse says, "A brother is born for adversity." We may think of siblings when we hear the word brother, but a brother could be a brother in Christ or a brother in the faith. The body of Christ is genuinely there for you, even in the worst of circumstances. Many times, trials help us see who our true friends really are, and we can form an even deeper friendship than family ties through adversity.

We have all, at some point in our lives, had a friend betray us, or we have had a friendship fizzle out, unable to withstand the hardships of life. A true friend who loves at all times is a precious gift. A true friendship, built on trust, loyalty, and wisdom from our Heavenly Father, is invaluable. It is priceless. As you explore these qualities of a true friend, ensure you embody them yourself and apply them to your own friendships. May we all be a priceless treasure to a friend in need.

Moment to Reflect:

- ♥ What characteristic of a friend means the most to you? Do you portray that characteristic in your friendships?
- ♥ Have you had a bad experience with a friend that left you afraid to put yourself out there again? You can use your experiences to know how to be a better friend to someone else.
- ♥ Do you need to evaluate some of your friendships to see if they are real or more like fake social media friendships?
- ♥ Ask God to help you be the kind of friend Solomon was talking about in this verse in Proverbs. Friendships are so important to build up believers and nonbelievers. Everyone deserves to have a friend.

Being a good friend is a ministry in its own right. By nurturing and supporting others, we demonstrate the love and compassion that Christ has shown us. It takes work, and we must be intentional in our efforts. As I realize who my true friends are, I need to recognize the warning signs of jealousy, envy, and deceit. True friendship is priceless, and I want to encourage and lift up the friends I have in my life.

Lord Jesus,

You are a true friend to me, and I want to be a true friend to the special people in my life. Help me to value honesty, trust, patience, reliability, and loyalty as I seek to form true friendships and be a true friend. I pray I will lift my friends up and comfort them during their tough times. Help me to be there in times of adversity and steer them back on the right path when they make wrong choices. I pray you will bring friends into my life who have all these same qualities of a true friend. They truly are priceless. Amen.

Friendship Has Sweet Rewards

---

*"The heartfelt counsel of a friend is as sweet as
perfume and incense."*
Proverbs 27:9 NLT

Have you ever walked by someone and thought, "Wow, I love that scent!" It was likely their perfume that triggered your senses and made you want to inhale deeply. Incense can often improve moods and even reduce stress and anxiety. It can also increase your calm and focus with a pleasant aroma, just like perfume. Proverbs 27:9 tells us how special friendship is and how it can affect us.

Heartfelt counsel means that your friend truly understands your situation, listens to your concerns with genuine care, and offers guidance rooted in honesty and love for Christ. When we have something going on with our kids, or we are struggling with the best way to parent in a certain situation, good counsel is so meaningful. These friends pray thoughtfully and seek wisdom from God before they advise you. They don't rush to offer opinions but instead carefully consider the best advice for you from a godly perspective. I have a friend like this, and it is the sweetest of friendships. She knows what is going on in my life, and she cares about what bothers me. When I have a certain view on an issue, she makes sure to get all the facts and gives me answers based on what God would want in my life, not what I would want. She listens when I need to vent about parenting concerns and prays over me and my kids in everything.

This kind of counsel is pleasing to God and invaluable in friendship and in motherhood. Motherhood is extremely rewarding but can also be stressful, demanding, and exhausting. A friend's counsel leaves a lasting impression on us as they listen, encourage, and advise, much like the impression perfume makes when someone enters and leaves a room. Their willingness to share our burdens, combined with their honesty and godly wisdom, helps us stay calm and focused, reducing our stress and anxiety, and enabling us to be the moms Christ wants us to be!

The next time you are in a store or an elevator, and you smell a sweet perfume, take a minute to remember Proverbs 27:9. As you encounter trials in your own life, I pray that you have a Godly friend who can give you heartfelt counsel—it truly is as sweet as perfume!

Moment to Reflect:

- ♥ Do you have a friend who provides you "heartfelt counsel" when you are going through a rough time as a mom? If not, ask God to provide someone in your life who can help you in that area.
- ♥ Do you have a favorite perfume or essential oil you like to diffuse? If you do, try to memorize Proverbs 27:9, and anytime you use your perfume or change your diffuser, think about this verse. Let your friend know how thankful you are for their counsel through your motherhood journey.
- ♥ Are you the kind of friend who jumps in and gives advice without being asked or praying about it? Try to think of ways to give godly counsel and ask God to give you opportunities to improve in this area.
- ♥ If you do have a godly friend who gives you heartfelt counsel, you may want to let them know how much you value them and how special they are in your life.

This verse takes on a whole new meaning when you think about the uses of perfume and incense and how they relate to self-confidence, stress, and anxiety. Having a friend who prayerfully considers options and seeks godly counsel before giving you advice is a rare and sweet thing. Let it make an impression on you, and don't ever take it for granted.

Lord Jesus,

I am grateful for friends who care about me and encourage me as a mom. I am most grateful for the ones who give me advice and counsel me after spending a great deal of time in prayer and seeking your will. They want to be honest but not give a rushed opinion about a problem. These friends are special because they care about my stress and anxiety and want to find ways to reduce it. Their Godly perspective provides a calm that can only come from you. Thank you for the sweetness of their friendship and the lasting impression it has on my life and the lives of my children! I love you, Jesus! Amen.

Friends Need Forgiveness

*"Bear with each other and forgive one another if any of you
has a grievance against someone.
Forgive as the Lord forgave you."*
Colossians 3:13

Thank goodness Jesus doesn't withhold forgiveness the way I try to forgive sometimes. The human side of me can be mean and want revenge. I don't want to turn the other cheek! I want to get even! It's a natural reaction when someone hurts us to want to retaliate. We want them to feel the same pain they caused us. Unfortunately, no matter how good it feels to picture them experiencing the same suffering they put us through, we must forgive. The very essence of forgiveness is extending favor (grace). When God extends forgiveness to us, he pardons (cancels) our debt whether we deserve the pardon or not. When someone wrongs us, and we choose to forgive, we're essentially letting go of that burden because it's too heavy for us to bear alone, and we aren't intended to carry it.

Forgiveness is hard, but bitterness will eat us alive. It destroys us from the inside out, making us difficult to be around. Holding a grudge hurts us more than it ever hurts the other person. If we choose not to forgive, our resentment of that person will continue to build, and we will live an endless cycle of bitterness mixed with anger and an urge to retaliate.

So, how do we stop this cycle? We must follow the example of Christ and forgive as He forgives us. Knowing that I am human, I also know that I am in constant need of forgiveness. Jesus gives it to me willingly the moment I ask. If I am forgiven for all I have done, why is it so hard to grant forgiveness to someone else for what they did or said to me? My children need to see me forgive. I don't want them to hold grudges and become bitter because they see me doing the same.

Guess what tends to happen when we choose to truly forgive someone? All those feelings of bitterness, resentment, irritation, and obsession start to fade away! I believe the phrase "fade away" is significant because, based on my experience, feelings do not disappear overnight. There could be hurt there that takes time to heal, but slowly, you recognize you aren't as angry and bitter as you used to be. My mom used to ask me to pray for the person I was bitter towards. It took me a long time to be able to do that. Her advice has come full circle, as I have passed on the same wisdom to my daughter! God helps us let go of those feelings and release the overwhelming heaviness that can consume us. It doesn't mean we condone bad behavior or even excuse it. It just means that we aren't going to let what they did destroy our hearts in the process!

Many situations are hard to forgive. Some people carry so much pain that it can be a struggle, but you don't want that pain to define your life. Forgiveness helps you recognize the pain but also heal from it slowly and emotionally. You can forgive but still hold someone accountable if they committed a crime. Forgiveness is simply releasing your grudge against them. It has nothing to do with justice and doing the right thing according to the law.

It's not easy to forgive when the other person feels no remorse. We still need to forgive for our own sake. Forgive because your children need to see true forgiveness. It's difficult to encourage forgiveness in our children when we are not willing to forgive. Forgiveness is essential in any relationship, but in friendships, it is what keeps us accountable and prevents resentment from damaging our connection.

Moment to Reflect:

- ♥ Have you ever been hurt badly and decided to harbor resentment instead of offering forgiveness? How did the resentment make you feel over time?
- ♥ Have you ever chosen to forgive someone when you didn't think they deserved it? Did choosing to forgive help you with your bitterness?
- ♥ Have you done anything to someone else that you need to ask forgiveness for? Pray for the courage to ask for forgiveness. It's the first step in healing the relationship.
- ♥ How does Jesus forgive you over and over when you mess up? When you want to hold bitterness against someone else, remind yourself that Jesus could do that to you, but He doesn't. It's not easy to forgive, but it is freeing.
- ♥ Is there anyone you need to forgive?

We focused on the forgiveness part of Colossians 3:13, but this verse is very relevant to friendships. In any relationship, there are going to be problems and times when one person hurts another. We must learn to be able to forgive in those times, or we will carry anger with us, and it will eat away at us, possibly affecting other relationships as well. Jesus is the ultimate example of forgiveness when you look at what He did on the cross. We will never suffer as He did, but we need to choose to forgive as He did.

Lord Jesus,

Forgiveness is hard for me. I struggle because I want to hold onto the anger, which grows until it consumes me. Can you help me get to a place where I can let go of the anger and be able to forgive? Can you help me to release the bitterness and resentment I feel and let my heart start to heal? It hurts when a good friend lets me down, but I don't want the bitterness I have to control me. Help me forgive them regardless of if I think they deserve it. Help me to set a good example of forgiveness for my kids. Jesus, thank you for forgiving me even though I don't deserve it, either. I love you, Jesus! Amen.

Let's Do Lunch

"Two are better than one, because they have a good return for their labor. If either of them falls down, one can help the other up. But pity anyone who falls and has no one to help them up."
Ecclesiastes 4:9-10

Ecclesiastes 4:9-10 paints such a wonderful picture of friendship. We aren't meant to go through life by ourselves. God created and placed friends in our lives to help us when we struggle, to laugh and rejoice with us in good times, to cry with us in sad times, to take care of us when we are weak, and to walk beside us always. When we try to go through life alone and turn away from others who want to help us, life can be a challenge. Without friendship, life can be lonely and much more difficult.

There have been times when we have had a loss in our family, or one of us had surgery, and our friends rallied around us, called, and brought meals to show they cared. I have had friends pick one of my kids up when I had to take one of my other kids to a game or an appointment, and it was a huge help to me. Sometimes, I have had a friend hug me, not even saying a word, but crying with me because they knew I was hurting, which hurt them, too. It is a powerful thing to stand in the gap for a friend and be the hands and feet of Jesus. It just proves that you don't even have to say a word to make a difference in someone's life. Showing empathy to someone through a hug or shared tears can reveal to them how much you care. You might be surprised by how much your children learn about being a good friend by observing how you treat your friends. They are watching and learning from us, so it is so important to be a good friend and a role model to your children.

Friends can also be good accountability partners in any aspect of your life. They can keep you on track for work, your faith, your marriage, a weight loss journey, an addiction problem, or even parenting issues. When we are tempted, we need someone to keep us accountable. When we are happy, we need someone to celebrate with us. When we are devastated, we need someone to encourage us and lift us up. No matter the situation, our purpose is to be there for others and love them as Jesus would.

The last part of verse 10 says, "Pity the man who falls and has no one to help him up." Nobody wants to be alone without friends to share life with. Our life is more fulfilling when we pursue a life of fellowship with others. Don't shut people out or push them away when they want to be involved in your life. Sharing life with others allows us to prioritize their needs and share the love of Christ as we minister to them during their time of need.

It's easy to get caught up in the busyness of life and neglect friendships along the way. Make an effort to reach out to the special people in your life who have been there for you. Make a lunch date, send a card or a text, catch a movie, take a walk, or meet for coffee, but most importantly, be available. God created us for fellowship!

Moment to Reflect:

- ♥ Have you had a difficult time in your life that was made easier by a friend?
- ♥ Can you think of two or three friends right now who would drop everything to be there for you if you needed them?
- ♥ How can you go about nurturing friendships to be the kind of friend others need and keep your friendships strong?
- ♥ If you have been shutting people out, what are some ways you can reach out to establish some good friendships? Think of at least three people to contact and reestablish friendships with.

Life can become so hectic and busy that we tend to push others aside and miss out on fellowship. We need to take the time to nurture these friendships with people that God created for us to do life with. If you have good friends, make sure they know you appreciate them. If you want good friends, ask God to provide the right ones in your life and invest in their lives, too. Friendship isn't one-sided. Be a friend. Everyone needs one.

Lord Jesus,

You created so many special people to come alongside me and help me in life. Thank you for each and every person who adds value to my life and joy to my days. I am blessed to have friends willing to stand in the gap for me when I am struggling. Help me to be a good friend and make time for others who need me. Let me never be too busy to be there for someone I love. I love you, Jesus. Amen.

Be Careful Who Your Friends Are

> "Do not be misled. "Bad company corrupts good character."
> 1 Corinthians 15:33

Friends are vital in our lives. They love us for who we are. They bring meals when someone is sick or has surgery. They cry with us when we are upset and laugh with us when we are happy. They help with our kids when we need to carpool. They serve as our accountability partners, forgiving us when we mess up, and providing counsel and advice as needed. They join us in prayer, lifting us up to Christ and consistently guiding us in His direction. There was a group of friends in Mark 2: 3-5 who literally lowered their paralyzed friend down to Jesus. They saw a need, and they found Jesus. They cut a hole in the roof of the house where He was preaching and lowered their friend down to Him. Jesus healed their friend because of their faith. Faithful, God-centered friends are vital in your life.

As you think about the people you hang around, do they have the same qualities as the types of friends mentioned above? Do they want what is best for you in life? Do they encourage you in your faith? Do they share your beliefs? According to 1 Corinthians 15:33, we must be very careful who we spend time with because bad company corrupts good character.

You could be a great person and a strong Christian, but associating with people of questionable character might negatively influence you, leading to doubts about your beliefs and decisions that contradict your faith. Initially, it may seem insignificant, as they gradually persuade you to make small compromises. As you begin to give into temptation, they slowly start getting you to compromise on other values until you don't even recognize yourself anymore or know what you believe.

Take a long look at your friendships. If you have friends who push you toward Christ, those are true friends who will help you make good choices. If you have friends who encourage you to make poor choices or get involved in things that don't align with your values, consider asking God for guidance in distancing yourself from those relationships.

Stay strong in your faith so you won't be misled. If you know what you believe and you stay strong in your values, it will be much harder for someone to corrupt you or your character. Make sure the friends you keep are the ones who lead you toward Christ and do not mislead you toward things of this world.

Moment to Reflect:

- ♥ Have you ever had a friend who got you into trouble often? What did you do about that friendship?
- ♥ In your life now, is there one friendship you may need to ask God to help you step away from for the sake of your character?
- ♥ What are some ways you can ensure that you are strong enough to step away when someone is trying to corrupt your character?
- ♥ Are you a good friend to others who need you? Can you ask God for ways to strengthen your faith and be a good friend?

It can be hard to step away if you have grown up with certain friends and are trying to turn your life around. How do you step away from people you have known for forever? With God's help. Ask God to give you direction and courage to be able to stand up for your faith and to put some space between you and those who may be misleading you. Friendships are important. Just be sure you are making the right ones!

Lord Jesus,

You created friends to be a blessing and a positive reinforcement in my life. Help me to have discernment as I choose who to spend time with. I pray that if there is anyone in my life who might lead me astray and cause me to compromise my core values, you will give me the strength to stand firm and distance myself from that person. Thank you, Lord, for wanting the best for me in my life. I love you, Jesus. Amen.

Where is Your Mission Field

"My command is this: Love each other as I have loved you. Greater love has no one than this: to lay down one's life for his friends. You are my friends if you do what I command."
John 15:12-14

D o we go out of our way to help others in need, or do we choose not to sacrifice time or money to help others? This verse in John 15 reminds us of what Jesus did for us and encourages us to do the same as we encounter certain situations. In this verse, Jesus' disciples have no idea what He is about to do or sacrifice for them. When Jesus proclaims, "No one has greater love than this," He is emphasizing that there is no greater love than the one He has shown to us. This love is an agape love, which means it is selfless. It puts someone else's good ahead of your own. The world's view of love focuses on what we can do to earn it or deserve it. You can't earn Jesus' love. It is unconditional.

Jesus gave up His life for us, but does He expect us to do the same? John 15:12-14 says, "he lay down his life for his friends." Perhaps Jesus doesn't mean death in the literal sense, but rather, dying to our sinful nature. Our old ways. We give up what we want for someone else. I think of missionaries who give up their own desires to serve others. They sacrifice time, comfort, finances, convenience, and even safety to show love to others who need Jesus. In my own life, I have been on several mission trips and had to raise money to finance my way. I sacrificed comfort, safety, and convenience so I could share Jesus with others. This impacted my life so strongly that I encouraged our children to go on mission trips with their youth group and family mission trips so they could see how to lay down their own desires to serve others.

Luke 10: 25-37 tells us the parable of the good Samaritan. This man took the time to help a wounded person on the side of a road and gave money to care for that person, even though he was a complete stranger. There was a priest and a Levite who passed this wounded man but did not stop to help. When we see people who need Jesus, and we are willing to give up our desires so they can know the love of Jesus, we are laying down what we want for a friend. Giving up our possessions and our time to someone who needs them is a selfless act of love. It isn't about what they can do for us; it's about the love we can show them through our actions. Imagine how different the church would be if we chose to serve and love others instead of demanding what we feel we deserve! Jesus deserved so much more, but He sacrificed all of it because He loved us that much.

In the last verse of our passage, Jesus said, "You are my friends if you do what I command." Jesus tells us that if we choose to be selfless and love others the way He showed love to us, we are His friends. He gave His life so others could see how much He loved them. Surrendering our desires or possessions to help someone else seems a small price to pay to spread the love of Christ. What an honor to be called a friend of Jesus.

Moment to Reflect:

- ♥ Have you had a difficult time in your life that was made easier by a friend?
- ♥ Can you think of two or three friends right now who would drop everything to be there for you if you needed them?
- ♥ How can you go about nurturing friendships and be the kind of friend others need to keep your friendships strong?
- ♥ If you have been shutting people out, what are some ways you can reach out to establish some good friendships? Think of at least three people to contact and reestablish friendships with.

If you have good friends, make sure they know you appreciate them. To find good friends, pray for God to bring the right people into your life and invest in those relationships. Friendship is a two-way street—be a friend to others because everyone needs one.

Lord Jesus,

I'm grateful for friendship. I'm thankful for people who would drop everything to be there for me if I needed them. I pray that I will be that kind of friend. I pray for you to help me to be selfless and compassionate in my friendships. I pray my children will see this compassion and learn to be that kind of friend to the people in their lives. I pray my heart will be softened to others' needs and that I will be the kind of friend I want to have. Thank you for creating friendships that help make a difference in our lives. I love you, Jesus. Amen.

Peace

"Mother's love is peace. It need not be acquired,
it need not be deserved."
–Erich Fromm

DAY 63

You're an Overcomer

"I have told you these things, so that in me you may have peace. In this world you will have trouble. But take heart! I have overcome the world."
John 16:33

Sweet mom who is stressed, worried, and completely exhausted: take heart. To the one who is holding on by a thread. The one who struggles with anxiety and feelings of inadequacy. The one who feels like her prayers aren't even reaching the ceiling. To the mom who is dealing with grief and sadness and needs comfort and encouragement, hold on. You will have peace again. You are an overcomer. How? Because you are a child of God, and your God is an overcomer!

Jesus never promised us that just because we believe in Him, we won't have troubles, heartaches, and valleys. He never promised us the easy road or a life with no sickness, death, or tragedy. He said that when we go through these things, take heart. Be confident and comforted in the fact that He has overcome the world. He has victory over death. He defeated it.

We can take our struggles to Him. They will not defeat us. We can take our fears to Him. They do not win. We can take our doubts, our pride, and our troubles and lay them at His feet. In the midst of our greatest trial, He will give us peace. He knows we will go through hard times, but He offers us peace and the assurance that He has conquered the world. We don't have to be afraid. No matter what we go through, He will walk through it with us, and He knows the peace that awaits us if we ask for it.

As moms, we are going to have days where we feel like our hearts are literally being torn into pieces. We are going to have doubts about our parenting and whether we made the right decision. We will hurt for our children when they hurt and worry over situations out of our control. God knows all of this and doesn't want us to go through it without hope. He wants to give us the peace that can only come from Him. Have you ever heard the phrase, "Calm before the storm?" I have shared with you in these devotionals about losing my sister. I was with her until her last breath, and at the time that should have broken me came the greatest sense of peace. That peace came from God, and He knew I needed it at that moment. He knew the sense of loss I felt, and He wanted me to know He was there. Some of you may have children who push you to the breaking point but don't lose hope. Each of these trials will strengthen us and hopefully push us to rely more on God. The important thing to remember is that we never have to go through trials alone.

Jesus knows this world can cause us despair, but He has overcome it. He can take our fears, worries, and stress because He knows what is waiting on the other side. Don't miss out on His peace by keeping your worries to yourself. Share them with Jesus, and let Him help you become an overcomer!

Moment to Reflect:

- ♥ Are you struggling with stress and worry and need to have peace in your life?
- ♥ Can you ask God to give you peace even in your trial, knowing He has defeated this world that brings us all the trouble?
- ♥ Can you use the situation you have overcome to encourage another mom or friend who may be going through something similar?

As moms, we all have times in our lives when we stress about our kids, ourselves, our spouse, our parents, siblings, and you get the idea. Wouldn't it be nice to have peace even when you were going through a trial? Don't go through it alone. Trust the one who has already overcome it.

Lord Jesus,

You endured more suffering than I hope I ever have to endure. I know as a Christian, I am not promised an easy life with no worries. But as a child of God, I am promised peace, and I need that in my life with all I have going on. Can you help me be an overcomer and experience the peace that only comes from you? I love you, Jesus. Amen.

God's Peace Doesn't Break the Bank

"Peace I leave with you; my peace I give you. I do not give to you as the world gives. Do not let your hearts be troubled and do not be afraid."
John 14:27

When Jesus spoke these words, He intended for us to have a peace that comforts us regardless of our circumstances. He understood that, as moms, we would encounter situations with our children that would make us anxious and fearful. No matter what age they are, this feeling never goes away. You can either let it eat at you until you make yourself sick, or you can accept the peace Jesus offers and experience calm despite what you are going through.

If everything is going well in your life, your kids are behaving, and no one is sick, you might find yourself experiencing a moment of peace. If you're feeling stressed, you might think that taking a vacation or a trip will provide some relief. It may give you momentary peace, but it never lasts. As believers, we will have suffering, misbehaving kids, and sick family members, but our peace doesn't depend on our circumstances. As a mother, there have been countless instances where I've allowed situations to worry me to the point of making me physically sick. I have gotten calls from other moms after certain instances took place within a group setting, and I worried about what part my child played. I have read texts on my kid's phones, and without context, I have worried about what they meant. My kids have been to places they were not supposed to be. They have lied to my face when I have asked them about something important. I'm not sharing this to blast their mistakes, but because I am a Christian mom trying to raise my very human children to love Jesus. They are going to make mistakes, and when they do, we still love them and point them to Jesus. To navigate the times when our children push us to our limits, we need the peace that only Jesus can provide. We can ask Him for it anytime.

I love the part of John 14:27 that says, "Do not let your hearts be troubled and do not be afraid." Jesus knows us well, doesn't He! He knew we would have anxiety and stress and borrow unnecessary trouble. He wanted to comfort us and tell us that we don't need to worry or stress because He has the peace to calm us in the storm. Only He can take a terrible situation and provide peace because we know He is still in control.

You can try to sail away, go to a spa, ski off a slope, or lie on a beach, but your problems will eventually find you no matter how far you go! The only way to truly have peace in your life is to allow Jesus into your life and let Him give you the peace you need. There are several ways to receive His peace.

Pray: You can spend time in prayers with God and ask Him to give you peace.

Listen: You can allow yourself to reflect on His promises, be still, and listen for Him to speak to you.

Study Scripture: You can look in the glossary of your Bible under the peace section and study each of the verses that speak about peace.

Daily Devotions: You can read a daily devotion that helps to center you and focus on God each day.

Peaceful Space: You can find a quiet space in your home to enjoy a calm moment.

Soothing Activities: Listening to soothing music or taking a walk in nature can also help you feel peaceful.

Breathing techniques: I always tell my kids to take deep breaths and just let out all the stress. I tell them this, especially before tests when they get anxious.

Journaling: Use a journal to write down everything you are grateful for. It helps to see how much you are blessed. Surround yourself with friends who are encouraging and will lift you up.

Supportive Friends: Join a prayer group or Bible study to regularly fellowship with like-minded people of faith.

Volunteer: Contact your church or other volunteer groups to find ways to serve others. This takes our focus off ourselves and allows us to think of others.

Rest: Make sure you rest. Sometimes, resting your body and your mind allows us to experience peace.

Let Go of Resentment: If you have any hatred or resentment toward anyone else, let it go. This unforgiveness makes it hard to have peace. It can only come from Him.

Try incorporating some of these practices into your daily life, and you'll notice a difference in your sense of peace. Don't spend one more day troubled or afraid.

Moment to Reflect:

- ♥ Have you ever tried to take a vacation to get away from your stress? How did that work out for you?
- ♥ Have you ever literally made yourself sick with worry over something because you couldn't let go and give it to God?
- ♥ Do you have anything now that may be bothering you or making you fearful? If you are a believer, don't let another day go by without asking God to give you peace. He wants you to have it.

Our children are everything to us. Whether your issues with your kids revolve around school, friend groups, dating, or driving, it is all scary. As they grow older and prepare to leave for college, the thought of them no longer living at home can be quite stressful. You may invent things that haven't even happened... but they could! Do NOT let your heart be troubled. I'm preaching to the choir here, but accept the peace Jesus offers and let your stomach settle. It's not worth an ulcer!

Lord Jesus,

I get so emotional when it comes to my kids. I only want what is best for them, but sometimes, I worry about things that may or may not happen. Please help me to accept the peace you offer to me and take my fear and worries away. I know that worry doesn't help me at all and can honestly make me physically ill if I let it continue. Thank you for the peace you give even during my trials. I'm thankful I don't have to take a vacation to get your peace. I love you, Jesus. Amen.

Rest Easy

"I will lie down and sleep in peace, for you alone, O Lord, make me dwell in safety."
Psalm 4:8 BSB

I believe all mothers would agree that we should embrace Psalm 4:8 and keep it in our hearts. If we could sleep peacefully without worrying about our baby's safety, our middle schooler's adjustment, our high schooler's curfew, or our college student's activities, it would truly be a miracle! Peace is a rare gift for a mom whose entire days are usually filled with chaos.

When I first read Psalm 4:8, I felt a sense of calm come over me just by reading it. I needed this verse when our first child was a baby. Every night, I would lovingly rock her to sleep and carefully lay her in her crib on her back. However, when I would return to check on her, she would always be lying on her stomach. I would continue to go back in and check on her to turn her back over. Every time I would go back, she would be on her stomach again! I was so worried about her that I wasn't getting any sleep. I was completely exhausted and scared. I called our pediatrician to ask him what to do. Being a Christian dad of three girls himself, he gave me some advice that I still remember to this day. He said, "Amy, if you don't get some sleep, you aren't going to be able to be the mom she needs you to be. You are going to have to lay her down and trust God to protect her and keep her safe." At the time, I didn't like that advice very much, but as the days went by, I realized he was right. I could not keep going on like this! I finally came to the point where I had a "come to Jesus" meeting. I prayed and told Him I was scared, but I asked Him to keep His hedge of protection around her while she slept. He did keep her safe, and I finally got some sleep! But it was hard to relinquish control. We need to remind ourselves that we are handing over control to the one who has been in control all along.

As I studied the background for Psalm 4:8, I realized King David probably needed to feel peace like I did. David's own son, Absalom, was trying to take over his kingdom, and it came to a point when David had to flee with all his officials, his wives, and his children. David was afraid for his life and was trying to keep all his people safe while trying to stop Absalom's revolt.

David went from a position of authority as king to wandering barefoot in valleys and over hillsides to stay ahead of Absalom's plans. He was scared for his own life and the lives of his wives and officials, and he also felt betrayed by his own flesh and blood. David's reasons were different from mine, but lying down during all this chaos could result in death for him and the loss of his kingdom if he wasn't careful.

Despite these circumstances, David knew that when he laid his head down, he could be at complete peace because the Lord Jesus would keep him safe. What a picture of love from our Heavenly Father to David when he needed it the most. Do we trust Jesus that much with our own lives? As you lie down tonight, know that Jesus has you and your children in His arms, and He wants you to sleep in peace.

Moment to Reflect:

♥ What can we learn from this story of David, as he was scared and unaware of what could happen to him?
♥ Do you have trials in your life that consume you and keep you from having peace?
♥ Will you commit Psalm 4:8 to heart and ask God to help you sleep in peace as you give your troubles and safety to Him?

It must have been heartbreaking for David to have to flee his kingdom with his family and officials to protect himself from his own son. All of us have situations in our lives that steal our joy and peace. Do you have the faith to reach out to God and receive the peace needed to rest and fulfill your calling as a mom?

Lord Jesus,

There is so much on my mind daily that it is hard to shut it off at night to rest. I know I worry about things that haven't happened or might happen when, in reality, they may never happen at all. I am weary and need rest so I can be the mom you have called me to be. Will you give me the peace that can only come from you and let me rest in that peace, knowing you will protect me and guard me from trouble? I love you, Jesus. Amen.

DAY 66

United in Peace and Unity

"Dear brothers and sisters, I close my letter with these last words; Be joyful. Grow to maturity. Encourage each other. Live in harmony and peace. Then the God of love and peace will be with you."
2 Corinthians 13:11 NLT

If you are trying to get your kids to do something, does encouragement or criticism work better for motivation? I have found encouragement works much better, putting them in a positive frame of mind versus constant reprimands, which can be discouraging and unproductive. When Paul wrote to the church in Corinth in 2 Corinthians, he wanted these believers living in a pagan world to have goals to strive for. He warned them on his last visit that he would not spare the ones who sinned when he returned. He wrote to them with the authority of the Lord behind him to give them a warning before he arrived. He wanted to build them up, not to tear them down.

In 2 Corinthians 12:20, Paul wrote that he feared he would find the Corinthians quarreling, jealous, having outbursts of anger, factions, slander, gossip, arrogance, and disorder. Wow. Every one of those characteristics is the exact opposite of peace! No wonder he wanted them to strive for full restoration, encourage one another, and live in peace.

Do any of you want your home to resemble a war zone? No one wants to live in a situation where there is quarreling, anger, jealousy, and disorder! How can we break free and live how Paul wanted the Corinthians to live? We need to strive for full restoration. When you restore something, you make it like new again or better than it is now. God can restore our lives to make them better and new if we ask Him to. 2 Corinthians 5:17 gives us that promise when it says, "Therefore, if anyone is in Christ, he is a new creation; the old has passed away; behold, the new has come." Everyone, especially children, thrives on encouragement, and Paul demonstrates how to use encouragement to create restoration. Being of one mind means not being divisive in our actions and purposely trying to cause dissension. We strive to create harmony in our household and let our faith help us be peacemakers.

When we strive to do all these things, like restoring and encouraging and being of one mind, we will be more at peace with fellow believers and hopefully nonbelievers as well. The last promise from our verse says that "the God of love and peace will be with you." If we strive for restoration, encourage others, and live in peace, God will be right there with us, leading us, guiding us, and showering us with His love and peace. What an awesome promise to know that we just need to strive with our hearts in the right place, and God will be there to cover us with peace.

Moment to Reflect:

- ♥ Does your life resemble the life of the Corinthians, or are you striving to live in peace?
- ♥ If you have quarreling, jealousy, and gossip in your home, are you ready to make a change to live in peace?
- ♥ Will you commit to praying for restoration in your own life, begin to encourage others in your daily life, and strive to be like-minded in your approach to situations?

Paul was striving to get the Corinthians back on track. He had warned them several times and didn't want them to live in jealousy, anger, and disorder. His suggestions of full restoration, encouragement, and living like-mindedly were meant to help them achieve a life of peace. We can learn so much from scripture to help us achieve the life God meant for us to have.

Lord Jesus,

I know I need to make some changes in my life to remove the obstacles interfering with my peace. I pray that you will fully restore me and help me turn away from my old ways and become new. I want to encourage my children and lift them up, and I want to be a peacemaker in all situations. I pray for peace in my life and that God will shower me with His love and peace as I trust in Him. Amen.

No Matter What

---

*"Do not be anxious about anything, but in every situation,
by prayer and petition, with thanksgiving, present your
requests to God. And the peace of God, which transcends all
understanding, will guard your hearts and your
minds in Christ Jesus."*
Philippians 4:6-7

Just in case you were wondering about a little background for this verse, let me shed some light on it for you. Paul wrote Philippians while he was imprisoned in Rome. Think about that for a minute. A person who was imprisoned for preaching the gospel is telling others not to be anxious about anything. Paul was in prison and telling others not to be anxious. How many times as a mom have I been anxious about something from the comfort of my home or car? I might worry about a situation with my child's teacher, stress over a test grade, be concerned that my child was hurt by a friend, or be terrified about my child driving. I can find myself worrying about any of these things, whether I'm sitting on the couch, waiting in the carline, or working behind a desk. I don't have to add to that worry by doing it in handcuffs behind bars. Paul valued prayer and his time with God no matter where he was.

He knew that even if he had to suffer, God would be with Him and never leave him.

Paul tells the church at Philippi to be thankful in every situation as they present their requests to God, not just when things are going their way or everything is perfect, but even on their worst days. As a mom who often lets anxiety creep in, I will repeat Philippians 4:6-7 to myself when I feel stressed and overwhelmed to help me calm down. God says, "in every situation," and I take that literally. It doesn't matter how small it is if it makes me anxious, I talk to God and ask Him for peace. You can help your kids learn this verse, too, so when they get anxious about a test, nervous about a tryout, or scared about a performance, they can say it to themselves and let God calm them.

Paul wrote this verse in Philippians from the perspective of someone who had personally experienced it. He had been in the worst possible situations. He had been stoned, left for dead, imprisoned, shipwrecked, and imprisoned again! Even my worst days as a mom don't look like Paul's! Most people who had been through that many trials probably wouldn't say, "Do not be anxious about anything," unless they had experienced the peace of God.

God's peace in certain situations is unexplainable except through Christ. Realistically, Paul shouldn't have been at peace when he was stoned, shipwrecked, and thrown in prison, but he was. God's peace guards our hearts and minds. A guard's duty is to protect, so when God guards our hearts and minds with His peace, He is providing mental and emotional protection for us. This peace can prevent us from being overwhelmed with our troubles. The last three words, "in Christ Jesus," are crucial. We can experience this peace exclusively through Christ Jesus. He gave His life for us, and if we believe in Him, we can enjoy the peace that Paul experienced.

Moment to Reflect:

- ♥ Do you tend to have anxiety over certain situations you face as a mom?
- ♥ How does learning all that Paul went through change your perspective on your anxiety?
- ♥ Will you hide Philippians 4:6-7 in your heart and pray to God with thankfulness, even if your situation is troubling? Ask God for His peace that passes all understanding.

Paul had every reason in the world to be anxious. He had repeatedly been through rough times, and yet he encouraged others not to be anxious. What a testimony to his faith! I struggle with anxiety when it comes to certain situations with my kids, and I need to step out in faith, knowing that God can handle any situation. He wants to give me His peace to calm my anxiety. What an awesome God!

Lord Jesus,

Having kids can bring on anxiety easily. We worry about a situation when we don't know how it will turn out, but Lord, you know the outcome. I pray that I will learn a lesson from Paul's suffering and learn to pray to you more and worry less. You want to protect us and guard us from anxiety. Help me to be thankful for your presence and trust in you for the peace that passes all understanding. Thank you for guarding my heart and my mind so I don't have to worry. I love you, Jesus. Amen.

Trusting Gives You Peace

"May the God of hope fill you with all joy and peace as you trust in him, so that you may overflow with hope by the power of the Holy Spirit."
Romans 15:13

It's not always as easy as it sounds to trust in God. We can't see what He sees. We see what is happening in our lives, and we worry, hurt, get angry, and panic. What if my child doesn't make the team? What if my daughter doesn't get picked for a special group for dance or cheer? What if this illness doesn't get better? What if my child makes this bad choice? We forget that God knows how it will turn out. He knows exactly when our situation will end, get worse, or get better. Paul wrote this verse in Romans because he wanted us to be filled with joy and peace. Paul, of all people, had many instances when it would have been extremely hard to trust, but he did. 2 Corinthians 11: 23-28 gives an account of all Paul suffered. He was whipped with 39 lashes (5 different times), beaten with rods (3 different times), struck with stones, shipwrecked (3 times), and survived dangerous rivers, robbers, Gentiles, and the wilderness. He had cold, sleepless nights filled with hunger and thirst, but in 2 Corinthians 4:17-18, he called all of these "light and momentary afflictions." God carried Paul through situations that would leave others defeated and bitter, but Paul was filled with joy and peace.

I don't know what you have been through as a mom, but I do know that being a mom is hard. As we care for these small humans as they grow, there are many instances where we must depend on our faith in God for our own peace of mind. I love that the first part of Romans 15:13 refers to God as "the God of hope." He cares for us and wants us to have hope and encouragement. He wants us to trust in Him, even if we can't see how He is working, He loves our faith.

You can either try to handle a trial on your own or you can trust in God. If you have a situation you are struggling with, you need joy and peace to carry you through it. As an added bonus, the Holy Spirit helps you overflow with hope. Hope gives you something to look forward to, gives you encouragement, and promises that your struggles are not going to last forever.

Romans 15:13 encourages us to trust in God when we have struggles and let the joy and peace He offers carry us through hard times. We can make it with His help, and we have hope straight from His Holy Spirit flowing through us as we lean on Him. He is a good God.

Moment to Reflect:

- ♥ Are you discouraged, trying to go through something without any help from God?
- ♥ When you are struggling, do you trust in God to give you joy and peace, or do you try to handle it on your own?
- ♥ Mom struggles are real, and our anxiety can become so intense that it affects our health. Put your trust in God when you are struggling, and let Him fill you with the joy and peace to get through whatever trial you are going through.

I am still amazed that Paul called our God "the God of hope" after all he had been through. He was a walking testimony of faith and a great example for us to follow when we are going through trials in our own lives. Even in dealing with major struggles, Paul put his trust in God, and God gave him joy, peace, and hope.

Lord Jesus,

Sometimes, I get so overwhelmed that I let my anxiety consume me, and I don't come straight to you with my troubles. Help me to trust in you when life gets me down, and fill me with the joy and peace that can only come from you. My circumstances may seem troubling, but I know that you are a God of hope, and I pray your Holy Spirit will help me overflow with hope. I love you, Jesus. Amen.

DAY 69

What Rules Your Heart?

"Let the peace of Christ rule in your hearts, since as members of one body you were called to peace. And be thankful."
Colossians 3:15

As a mother, you make countless decisions every day, and each one is influenced by your deep love and strong desire for their safety and well-being. Sometimes, concern can morph into overwhelming worry and anxiousness. Pride can also play a role, prompting you to try to control every aspect of your child's life, inadvertently limiting the space for God's guidance. The busyness of managing various activities may also crowd out opportunities to pause, reflect, and discern what God might be directing you toward. Taking time to slow down and listen to your inner guidance can be essential amidst the hectic pace of parenting.

There are so many things that can rule our hearts if we let them. Fear is a big one for moms. We let fear rule, and we get anxious about situations that may never happen. We must have faith that God will protect our children and watch over them. To me, the exact opposite of fear is peace. Peace doesn't happen automatically. We need to decide to let it take control of our hearts.

If our hearts are bitter, selfish, and ungrateful, there is no room for peace to rule. There are many factors that can lead us towards bitterness or ingratitude, but we must counter these with feelings of gratitude and joy. As mothers, it's challenging not to compare ourselves to other moms or our families to others. Social media often tempts us to scroll through and see everyone's highlights, yet we don't witness what's happening behind the scenes. It's easy to pass by a post and wish for vacations, invitations, or luxuries others seem to have without knowing their marital struggles, parenting challenges, or financial burdens. Instead of comparing, I need to pause, thank God for my blessings, and recognize how truly fortunate I am.

If we are walking in Christ and choosing to follow Him daily instead of our own desires, then God's peace should flow freely in our hearts. It doesn't mean we won't experience heartbreak and grief, but when we do experience hard times, we will have a peace in our hearts that passes all understanding.

The last three words of the verse are "And be thankful." Don't discount them because they are only three words or because they are mentioned last. They are very important. When your heart has lost all thankfulness, and you aren't grateful for all God has blessed you with, it is impossible for peace to rule in your heart. When we are thankful for God's grace, and we know that He works everything for our good, it allows us to have peace.

As Christians, we are called to peace. Trust in God and be thankful and grateful for all He has blessed you with and all He has done for you. Get rid of bitterness and pride and choose to spend time with God daily. If you do these things, the peace of God will rule your heart.

Moment to Reflect:

- ♥ Are you struggling to have peace in your life? Do you have any bitterness, pride, or ungratefulness you need to get rid of?
- ♥ What is ruling your heart right now? If it's not peace, what can you do to change that?
- ♥ Are you thankful in your life? As a mom, you probably have a lot to be thankful for. Tell God all you are grateful for and ask for peace to rule your heart.

God made us to be at peace, so if you aren't feeling very peaceful, do a reality check. Are you thankful for all you have? Are you grateful for what God has blessed you with? Is there anything in your life, such as bitterness, pride, or fear, that is overtaking your chance for peace? Talk to God and work it out. He wants you to be at peace.

Lord Jesus,

I don't want to let anything else take the place of your peace in my heart. I want it to rule my heart and take over in the middle of my struggles and pain so I can feel your presence. Help me to spend time with you daily and grow closer to you. Help me to always be thankful for all you have given me in my life. Thank you for the promise of peace even in my worst moments. Help the peace that rules my heart overflow from me to others so your love will reach those who need it. Amen.

Purpose

"Successful mothers are not the ones that have never struggled, they are the ones that never give up, despite the struggles."
–Sharon Jaynes

Change of Plans

---

*"Commit to the Lord whatever you do, and he
will establish your plans."*
Proverbs 16:3

So often, I start out trying to do things my way, and I think I have it all under control until everything goes haywire. I think stubbornness with a little pride mixed in makes me think I can handle things by myself, and I don't need to bother God with it. But He wants me to ask for help. He wants me to call on Him.

Sometimes, the unknown can be a little scary, and it's hard to give up control and ask for help. It may be hard to commit to the Lord if you think he will change your plans or make you alter the course you think is best. He may have a different plan in mind that is greater than you would have ever imagined for yourself. When I was in college, I had this great job that I thought would be perfect for me for the summer and would have been great on my resume. I could also live on campus and not have to drive very far to commute. Unfortunately, my dream job did not work out, and I ended up working at a different job that summer that had nothing to do with my major or future career. I did not understand why the other job didn't work out until the end of the summer. I met a certain guy at this job that summer that I started dating. Even though that job wasn't in the career path I wanted for my future, it was in the path God wanted for my future. It has been 28 years since that summer job, but that special guy and I have been married for 26 years. It was hard for me to see the reasoning behind why the other job fell through, but God had a different purpose in mind. Many times, our desires change when we put Him first, and what we now value is His purpose for our lives.

Proverbs 16:3 not only applies to us as moms, but we can also teach it to our kids to encourage them to include the Lord in their plans. When we include the Lord, He takes the lead, and we follow. We exchange our will for His. This verse applies to our child's classes, jobs, dating relationships, or friendships. When you commit to something, you entrust yourself completely to it, working hard with determination and discipline. When you commit to the Lord, your faith may be tested when certain plans are beyond your control, but you allow God to guide you. Allowing God to guide you ensures that your plans will succeed because you are committed to Him and His will. God's view of "success" may be different from your own. Many times in my own life, God's plan for me was so much better than my own. If we seek Him and commit all we do to Him, He will get the glory, and we will be a success!

As you commit Proverbs 16:3 to memory and hide it in your heart, take a moment to think about the person who wrote it. Soloman, the wisest man to ever live on the earth, thought it important enough to include this verse in the book of Proverbs. If you want to be a wise mom and have your plans succeed, you need to take every success, every plan, every question, and even every failure to God daily. You can't just go to Him with the big things. He wants you to trust Him with the little things, too. Surrendering doesn't have to feel like you are losing something. When you are tempted to make your own plans, and you don't want to let go, instead of thinking of it as surrendering, think of it as seizing something more unshakeable than control: God's will. When I relinquish control to God, I don't have to worry about the future because I know that my plans will align with His will for me.

Moment to Reflect:

♥ Looking back on decisions you have made in the past that didn't turn out as you had hoped, why do you think they may have failed?

♥ When you make plans or have a decision to make, are you eagerly anticipating the future and all its possibilities or scared to death of the unknown? If you are fearful, have you committed your plans to God or forging ahead on your own?

♥ How can you change the way you handle plans going forward to ensure they are blessed with success?

The wisest man in the world wrote a verse just for us that promises our plans will succeed if we commit them to the Lord. Why would we venture out on our own with no knowledge of the future just to say we did it by ourselves? I want my plans, hopes, and dreams to succeed, and I want to be in God's will and let Him direct my steps. I'm so grateful for this promise from the Bible that gives me hope when I trust and commit to Him.

Lord Jesus,

I have failed so many times in the past by choosing my own way. You know the future, and I know you want what is best for me. Help me to trust in you and commit my plans to you in everything I do so that they will succeed. I pray for my children as well that I will share this verse with them and help them to hide it in their hearts so their paths will be directed by you. Thank you, Jesus! Amen.

What Purpose Will You Be Known For?

"But I have raised you up for this very purpose, that I might display My power to you, and that My name might be proclaimed in all the earth."
Exodus 9:16 MSB

The screaming cries of a baby in a river filled with alligators, snakes, and only a basket to separate him from the dangerous water: this was how Pharaoh's daughter found baby Moses! God had a purpose for his life, just like He has a purpose for yours. Moses' purpose was to rescue the Israelites from Pharaoh through a mass exodus. The word exodus literally means "a mass departure of people," and with Moses rescuing more than two million Israelites, it definitely fits the description! God allowed Pharoah to be in the position he was in at that point in time for a reason. God works through people, and even though He doesn't have to use us to accomplish His purpose, He chooses to. You may have gone through something traumatic growing up or in early adulthood that prepared you for the position you are in now. You may be the only one who can confront a boss or leader, or you may be the leader who is able to use their influence in a positive way.

Not only does God choose the least likely people to accomplish His plan, but He also empowers them to achieve remarkable things, demonstrating that His strength is made perfect in our weakness. God chose Moses even though Moses had a speech problem and did not want to be in front of people. God had other plans and allowed Moses to lead these two million out of Egypt and toward the promised land. Pharoah had multiple opportunities to save his people and himself, but he chose to be stubborn, and it cost him dearly.

I felt God calling me to be a counselor at a crisis pregnancy center, even though I had never experienced any of what these women had gone through. I felt completely unqualified, but I got the courage to get the training I needed and made myself available. I was able to counsel multiple women into choosing life for their babies. I was married and pregnant with our first child, so I got special permission to use my ultrasound video instead of a random one they use with the clients. God took my willingness and used me for a greater purpose. The clients I spoke to could relate to me because I was pregnant, too, but they saw my heart for God and my heart for the life inside me, and God used that to change lives.

I doubted I had anything to offer, but God said otherwise. Moses doubted himself but was willing to be used by God to fulfill His purpose. God wants to work through us in mighty ways we can't even imagine, but we must submit to Him and His plans for us. When we become willing vessels like Moses, we contribute to God's plan and experience a deeper connection with Him. The sad truth is that Pharoah, in all his power, still paid the ultimate cost by losing a child because of his stubbornness.

As Christian moms, may we learn from Pharoah's mistakes. God has put us in the position we are in for His purpose. We can seek His purpose by reading our Bible, praying for direction from Him, and always trying to seek His will. We can worship Him through singing and praising, and we can fellowship with other believers and allow them to lift us up and encourage us in our faith. We are to honor Him and teach our children to love Him. We can choose to be willing and available for God, allowing Him to achieve great things through us, or we can go our own way and miss out on the blessings He wants to give us. What purpose would you like to be known for?

Moment to Reflect:

- ♥ Have you hardened your heart like Pharoah, not believing that you need Him to accomplish His purpose?
- ♥ Do you make excuses as Moses did with his speech problems when you know God is calling you to accomplish something through Him?
- ♥ Have you noticed when you say yes to God for small things, He continues to use you for bigger things?

Moses was the last person anyone thought would lead two million people out of Egypt, but God thought otherwise. Don't ever doubt what God can accomplish through you if you allow Him to. If you find yourself in a position of privilege and power like Pharoah, make sure that your pride doesn't make you lose sight of the power of God and the means He will use to accomplish His purpose.

Lord Jesus,

I often come up with excuses for why I don't feel qualified to carry out Your plans through me. Please help me be willing to say "Yes" whenever You call. I don't want my heart to become stubborn like Pharaoh's. I pray that I will be open to saying "Yes" even to the small things so You can trust me with the bigger tasks. You created and saved me, and I have a special purpose in Your plan. Please help me always remember that. Amen.

Stepping Stones of Life

---

*"For we are God's workmanship, created in Christ Jesus to do
good works, which God prepared in advance as
our way of life"*
Ephesians 2:10 BSB

I have to be honest; sometimes, I struggle with feeling worthy. I subconsciously compare myself to other moms and other women and feel like I don't measure up. To some extent, all of us tend to compare ourselves to others and strive to achieve unrealistic goals that were never ours to attain. This verse from Ephesians 2:10 tells us that we are God's handiwork, His artistry, His masterpiece. When we were saved, Christ Jesus placed His Holy Spirit in us and created a new version of us. Through our decision to follow Christ, we can carry out God's plan and do good works for Him. God already has a plan for what we are supposed to accomplish, and we don't have to try to achieve the same goals as someone else. Those goals are God's plan for them, not us.

When we were saved, we were given special and unique gifts and abilities. These abilities are God's way of continuing to shape us and use us to further His kingdom. God created a path for our lives and gave us the tools to set foot on that path and make a difference for His kingdom. You are reading this book today because God gave me a gift to write! He put this desire in my heart and wanted me to share my gift with others by writing what He wanted me to say. When we doubt ourselves, we are doubting God's ability to provide us with exactly what we need to accomplish His purpose in our lives.

My background, trials, lessons, and accomplishments shape my unique ability to contribute in specific situations. My good works and how I can reach people may be completely different than how God uses you, but we can both accomplish His goals if we choose to follow Him.

If you feel like God isn't using you right now, be patient. Make sure you are where you need to be in your relationship with Christ. Are you spending time with Him daily? Are you praying, reading His word, and listening to what He wants to say to you? Are you surrounding yourself with fellow Christians who can build you up and encourage you in your faith? He may be starting out small. I volunteered as a Christian counselor for a while and then was asked to lead prayer groups at my church for special events, where I had to present the plan of salvation and pray with strangers. From there, I was asked to teach Sunday School in our children's department and taught for nine years. Each encounter was a stepping stone that led me to the next opportunity, giving me the experience I needed to help me in my next mission.

Think about the story of David from the Bible and how he worked his way up to power. We look at David and see a king. God looked down and saw a shepherd first. The skills David learned as a shepherd helped him defeat the giant Goliath. When David conquered Goliath, it gave the people confidence in him to fight other battles until God decided he was ready to be king. God prepared your good works ahead of time, just like David. He will work through you in His time. Remember, you are a masterpiece!

Moment to Reflect:

- ♥ Are you making your relationship with Christ a priority so He can use you to accomplish great works?
- ♥ Have you given up too soon or gotten frustrated with God because you are comparing your experience to someone else's? He uses us all at different times, and you could be in the "Shepherd phase," while those you are comparing could be in the "King phase." God's timing is not our timing.
- ♥ Make it a priority to focus on your prayer time and quiet moments, read and study God's Word more frequently, listen for His guidance, and surround yourself with Christian friends who will support and encourage your faith. Be ready for God to do incredible things in your life.

David is such a great example from the Bible of what we can look forward to when God uses us for His good works. David had to be patient and wait on God's timing. Some of the skills he needed to learn took time and seemed unimportant at first. God always has a plan and has your best interest at heart. Wait for His timing, and know you were created to do good works!

Lord Jesus,

I don't have to doubt myself or compare myself to anyone else. You made me unique and created me for a specific purpose. Help me to always seek you and grow in my faith so you can use me for the good works you have already planned. Every experience I go through is a stepping stone, guiding me to where You want me to be and helping me achieve what You have in store for me. I love you, Lord. Amen.

Moldable To the Maker

"Delight yourself in the Lord, And He will give you the desires of your heart. Commit your way to the Lord, Trust also in Him, And He will do it."
Psalm 37:4-5

Would you agree that the people you know best are the ones you spend more time with? If I spend several hours a week with certain people, I'm going to get to know what they like, their views, their favorite food, drink, phrases, personality traits, bad habits, and much more. If I enjoy spending time with them, I want to be part of their life and know their dreams and goals, and celebrate their joys with them. The same is true with us and God. If we want to know Him more, we need to spend time with Him. We listen to Him and know what makes Him happy and what makes Him disappointed. We show our awe of Him and His creativity by getting up to watch a sunrise or being out in nature and listening to the birds chirp and seeing the beauty of a sunset, green grass, the mountains, the ocean, the forests, the streams, the waterfalls and everything in between. We talk to Him by praying and telling Him our struggles, our hurts, and our dreams. We make Him a priority! He created us because He wanted to have fellowship with us.

Do you know why the Bible is sometimes referred to as God's Word? It's because it is. The Bible is God-breathed, which means He spoke the words, and the prophets wrote them down and recorded them for us to read thousands of years later. Many of us don't read our Bible because we either don't understand it or maybe it just seems too old to apply to us today. You can't just read a verse or two, close your Bible, and expect God to speak to you. He wants you to read it, meditate on it, and commit the verses to memory so you can apply it in your life. I journal in my Bible and write little notes about what was going on at the time. Months or even years later, I turn the page and see my notes and remember how God got me through that time in my life.

Even more than reading His word, we need to live it! He gave us His thoughts about parenting, discipline, marriage, forgiveness, injustice, money, relationships, temptation, waiting, worry, and many more. You can look in the glossary at the back of your Bible and find the subject you need to read about. Reading His word is vital to knowing Him more, but living it out is how we draw closer to Him. The Bible calls David a man after God's own heart. If you know anything about David's story, he made some bad decisions in his life. God loved David because David delighted in God. He worshiped Him, sang to Him, and spent time truly pouring his heart out to God. He showed God he loved Him by his actions. He wasn't a perfect man, but he strived to know God more and honor Him in his actions.

As we delight in Him, we allow ourselves to be molded into who He wants us to be. Our hearts become more in tune with Him, and when we are in tune with Him, our desires are aligned with His will for our lives. Psalm 37:4 never promises that we will get everything we desire if we delight in the Lord, but it does promise that when we delight in His presence, our desires begin to change. Our new desires are His desires for us.

Like any friendship or mentorship, the more time we invest with someone, the greater their impact and influence on us becomes. The more I worship Jesus and listen to Him through prayer, the clearer I hear His desires for my life and find myself aligning my will with His intentions for me. I no longer want what I wanted for myself. I now want what He wants for me.

When we combine delighting in His presence with committing our ways to Him, we can expect Him to move with purpose. Committing our ways to the Lord means surrendering our choices, actions, plans, and the direction we want our lives to follow. Our purpose as moms should be to delight in the Lord and be moldable for Him to use us in our children's lives. As we commit our ways to Him, our purpose and His purpose become in sync, and we are right where we are supposed to be in His will.

Moment to Reflect:

- ♥ Are you taking time to spend time with God? Don't just check the box. Allow Him to speak to you and truly listen. Spend time praising Him.
- ♥ Think about your plans, your choices, and your actions. Are you committing them to Christ?
- ♥ Make an effort to be moldable so the Lord can use you. If you are rigid or set in your ways and unwilling to change for Christ, He can't shape you into who He wants you to become.

When we give our desires to God, we are showing Him that we want to be perfectly aligned with His plans. God knows our hearts as moms, and He knows the desires we have for ourselves and our children. If we are in His will, we will thrive as moms because that is exactly where He wants us to be. Being in the center of His will means we are putting Him first, and we are choosing to be the moms He wants us to be. When we commit our plans to Him and we spend time letting Him shape our lives, our desires will run parallel with His. Our purpose will be part of His plan, and we will be much more content than we ever would have been with wealth and material possessions.

Lord Jesus,

Help me carve time out for you each day so that you can mold me and make me into who you want me to be. I want my desires to be your desires. As I commit my plans to you, I pray that you will reveal your purpose for me and allow me to accomplish everything you desire me to accomplish as a mom. Amen.

Be a Blessing and Build the Kingdom

"God has given each of you a gift from his great variety of spiritual gifts. Use them well to serve one another."
1 Peter 4:10 NLT

Have you ever received a unique gift for a birthday or special occasion, and you weren't entirely sure how to use it? There are many electronic devices and gadgets that come with instructions for us to know their exact purpose. If you throw these instructions away or only use part of them, you won't know the full extent of what they can do. You miss out on something great because you didn't want to take the time to learn how to use the gift.

A fan is meant to keep you cool. You can choose to keep it in the box or put it on a shelf, but if you are hot, you will want to plug it in and use it! A blender can help make delicious smoothies, and a set of headphones can let you listen to music without disturbing those around you, but none of these are of any value if we don't use them. They also don't work without a source of power. They need to be "plugged in" to work or charge enough to be used. We need to be "plugged in" to

God so we can receive His power and be able to use our spiritual gifts. There are many gifts God has given us to use, and many times, we treat them like the fan, the blender, or the headphones. We put them on a shelf or never turn them on, and others miss the benefits that our gift can provide!

When we become Christians, God gives us spiritual gifts that are unique to us. In our verse for today, 1 Peter 4:10, God instructs us to use whatever gift we have received to serve others. We weren't meant to keep our gifts on a shelf. The purpose of our gifts is to benefit others. God blessed me with the gift of exhortation, which involves offering encouragement and support to help others fulfill their potential. I express this gift through my blog and newsletter, consistently writing encouraging posts guided by God. He also gave me the gift of hospitality. I didn't realize this was a gift until several people, at different times, told me I had blessed them through hosting them! Hospitality is the ability to make people, including strangers, feel welcome in your home to serve them.

There are people God has equipped with a gift for teaching, evangelism, leadership, serving, etc. God chose you for a purpose: to have the gift *you* have been given! You were meant to use your gift to be a blessing to someone else. When you use your gift, others are blessed, and it brings glory to God. Using your gift can help build up the kingdom for Christ. If you know you have a special gift, and you have been keeping it on the shelf, it's time to dust it off and put it to use. You are denying someone else the joys of the gift God gave you. Be a blessing!

Moment to Reflect:

- ♥ If you are a believer, are you using the spiritual gift God gave you when you became saved?
- ♥ Can you think of others you know who have blessed you with their gifts? Let them know how much they have touched your life.
- ♥ Examples of some spiritual gifts include the gift of service, the gift of teaching, the gift of encouragement, the gift of giving, the gift of leadership, the gift of kindness, the gift of faith, and the gift of discernment. For a comprehensive list of spiritual gifts, refer to Romans 12 and 1 Corinthians 12.

What a wonderful chance we have to bless others by using the gifts God has specifically given us. It would be such a shame to leave them on a shelf and deny others that blessing. Pray and ask God to show you what your gift is. He wants you to use it for Him.

Lord Jesus,

Thank you for blessing me with my own unique gift. Help me find ways to use it for your glory so I can be a blessing to someone who needs it. Help me realize it's not about me. It's about you and how I can help further your kingdom. I want to use this gift to fulfill my purpose in your plan for my life. Give me the courage and strength to take it off the shelf and use it for you! Amen.

How to Make God Laugh

"Many are the plans in a person's heart, but it is the Lord's purpose that prevails."
Proverbs 19:21

Can you picture the pearly gates of heaven shaking from the vibrations of uncontrollable laughter as God tries to compose Himself after we tell Him our plans? It may sound extreme, but it's absurd to make plans without seeking God's guidance to ensure we're aligning with His will for our lives! As moms, we have so many choices to make daily. Many of these involve our children and their well-being. Sometimes, we don't even stop to consult God or wonder if the plans we make are part of *His* plan. Even if we have the best of intentions, if we are outside of God's plan, it will most likely end in disappointment. Proverbs 19:21 brings comfort by reminding us that we don't have to rely on ourselves to make plans because His purpose will prevail.

I tend to be a little bit of a control freak. I like to have everything planned out and know exactly what is going to happen. The joke that says, "If you want to make God laugh, tell Him your plans," really helps my perspective. It is extremely difficult for me to delegate because I know if I do it, whatever "it" is, I will do it to the best of my ability, and it won't be finished until it is perfect. When God is in the picture, I don't have to worry if it will be done to perfection because the work is being done by God, and He *is* perfection! As "Type A" as I am, and as much as I like control, when it comes to my future and the future of my family, I want the Lord in control… not me.

Is it wrong for us to have plans? Not necessarily. If we are in tune with God and we are letting His Holy Spirit lead us, then it could be God who is nudging us to make a certain decision or have a certain idea. He may have laid it on our hearts. We can have dreams and plans, but we just need to make sure that our plans align with God's will.

The ability God gives us to make our own choices is very freeing, but it can also be overwhelming. When you have a decision to make, seek direction from God and allow Him to guide you toward the right path. As His plans unfold, you will realize His purpose is always to seek what is best for you and to bless you with an eternal perspective in mind. Many times, His best may not look like a blessing in the moment. He tells us in Isaiah 55:8, "For my thoughts are not your thoughts, neither are your ways my ways," declares the LORD. He may have His own way of accomplishing His purpose, but His will is always for our good.

With each new day, as you make plans for your children, remember you are a child of God, and He also wants what is best for you. Pray constantly, listen for His Holy Spirit to guide you, rely on trusted mentors to give you Godly advice, and trust God as you make your decisions. Know that His purpose is always for your good.

Moment to Reflect:

- ♥ Do you pray about plans and seek God's direction before you make them?
- ♥ Have you been caught up in the enemy's lies as you struggle to make plans work? Focus on God's will, and your desires will match with His. We don't have to guess when we can consult the One who knows what to do.
- ♥ Have you been thrown a curveball? Many of us don't like change and sometimes, God likes to get us out of our comfort zone. Always remember the last part of verse 21: "His purpose prevails."

As moms, we are challenged with making numerous plans daily. As much as we may like control, we need to realize that God is the one who gave us these children to take care of. He also has their best interest at heart. Learn to rely on Him as you make plans. You are delegating to the Creator of the universe. If you have to give up control, I can't think of a better person to give it to!

Lord Jesus,

I struggle with wanting to be in control and directing the path I take. Help me to remember that you have gone before me to pave the way, and you want to keep me from bumps along the way. As I make plans, help me to trust in you for direction, knowing your purpose is always for my good. I love you, Jesus. Amen.

His Purpose is Always For Your Good

"And we know that in all things God works for the good of those who love him, who have been called according to his purpose."
Romans 8:28

I love God, so things are always going to work out for me, and I don't ever have to worry about bad things happening!

Oh, How I wish that were true! Romans 8:28, at first glance, makes you feel all warm and fuzzy, but just because God works for good does not mean that we won't experience heartache, tough times, or health issues. This verse in Romans is a promise to us as believers that even when we experience rough times, God will use those times to bring good into our lives and into the lives of those who love us. Sometimes, these tough times may touch strangers who are watching how we react even though we don't even know them. God can use tragedies to touch the lives of unbelievers.

Our family has been touched by cancer, and we have experienced heartache and loss, but we also saw so many ways that God worked throughout that time to reach others and let them see the love of Christ. My younger sister was only 41 when she went to be with Jesus. She touched many lives in the short time she was on this earth. We could choose to be bitter at God taking her when she had her whole life ahead of her, or we could trust Him. We could trust that He had a greater plan. The way we chose to celebrate her life and our confidence that she is in heaven gave others hope that we have something to look forward to after this life. They saw our faith as a testimony that even in the hard times, we will trust that He knows best.

I know how hard it is to be strong when you don't understand, but our kids need an anchor that holds them to their faith. Our purpose as Christian moms is to make sure we stay close to Christ, to surround ourselves with Christian friends who will build us up and encourage us, and to lift up our children daily and point them to Jesus. We will have times when we fall to our knees and cry out to God, but even on our knees, we know He has a plan, and it's for our good. We can always trust in His unwavering character despite our circumstances.

This world can be overwhelming, stressful, and mean, but we have the best news of all. Jesus has conquered this world. We know we will have struggles along the way, but He promised us that in all things, He is working for our good. Good will come out of the circumstance, no matter how bad it may seem.

Never lose sight of the hope we have in Christ. He is working for you. He is fighting for you. His purpose is always for your good. Trust Him in your heartache. Reach out to Him in your despair. How you handle a situation could be the reason someone else comes to Christ. Moments are never wasted with God.

Moment to Reflect:

- ♥ Does this devotion make you think about Romans 8:28 differently than you have before?
- ♥ Have you had instances in your life when you have seen God take a tragedy and use it for good?
- ♥ If you think about certain tough situations you have experienced, did you handle them in a way that would bring others to Christ or turn them away?

Moms are under a microscope sometimes when it comes to tough situations. Our kids look to us to set a good example, no matter the circumstances. All we can do is try to stay close to God and rely on Him to lead us, guide us, and direct us to make the right choices.

Lord Jesus,

I know that all things work for the good of those who love you, but I also know that I am not immune to heartache. Please help me to show the love of Christ in my actions and reactions so that anyone looking in will see Christ through me. I know your purpose is always for my good. Help my faith in you show even in tough times. Amen.

Worth

"There is no greater good in all the world than motherhood.
The influence of a mother in the lives of her children
is beyond calculation."
—James E. Faust

More Precious Than Silver or Gold

"For you know that it was not with perishable things such as silver or gold that you were redeemed from the empty way of life handed down to you from your forefathers, but with the precious blood of Christ, a lamb without blemish or defect."
1 Peter 1:18-19

Today's verses tell me that I am so valuable to Jesus that He didn't use silver or gold to redeem me from my sin but His own blood. Sometimes, we hear the word "redeemed," or we even see it in Scripture, but don't stop to think about what it actually means. "Redeemed" means to compensate for the faults of someone, atone, or make amends for evil. We have all sinned, and God can't be in the presence of sin. Jesus dying was the only way to pay for the things that you and I have done. I don't feel worthy enough for someone to die for me, but Jesus says I am.

Do you realize how special you are to God? Do you see speakers, musicians, and evangelists and think that God loves them more? If you ever question how much you are worth to God and how valuable you are, you only need to look at the cross. When God created our world, there was no sin. Adam and Eve had a great friendship with God and walked and talked with Him, but they brought sin into the world when they disobeyed God. God is so Holy that He could not be around sin, but He craved a friendship and relationship with each of us. He came up with a plan to offer the ultimate sacrifice for all sin so our relationship with Him could be restored. For sin to be forgiven, a pure and blameless sacrifice had to be made. In Biblical times, people would sacrifice their most spotless lambs to atone for sins. God knew that for each of us to be able to join Him in Heaven, there had to be the ultimate sacrifice. Someone so pure and blameless who could take on all the sins of the world from the time of Adam even until now. Jesus, God's son, was the only one who was pure and blameless in God's sight. God gave His only son to die on the cross so all our sins could be forgiven.

The precious blood of Christ redeemed you from a lifetime separated from God. Although God has every jewel at His disposal, not one of them would come close to what Jesus' blood was worth. Jesus died because I am worth it. He loved me enough that He wanted me in Heaven with him one day. I am priceless. You are priceless.

If you ever begin to doubt how much you matter to God, remember what Jesus went through on the cross. He could have easily called the angels to get Him down, but He didn't. He knew He had to die on that cross to fulfill God's plan to save us. He was willing to do that for you and for me because He considered us worth it. Don't ever doubt your worth.

Moment to Reflect:

- ♥ Do you struggle with your worth or value or think you are not important or that you don't matter?
- ♥ Think about this powerful event that happened on the cross and know that Jesus stayed on that cross for you.
- ♥ Whatever you are struggling with as a mom, God wants to help you through it. He has already proven how much He cares for you. Let Him help you through your struggles and seek that peace that can only come from Him.

As I was writing this devotion, the magnitude of what Jesus did for me caused me to pause and shudder with chills! When you stop and truly think about the sacrifice God made just to have a relationship with us, it is overwhelming. I am more precious than silver or gold to God. He values me, and Jesus has the nail-scarred hands to prove it.

Lord Jesus,

There is no way to read these verses and this devotion and think about what you did for me and not be blown away. I am so very grateful that you considered me worthy enough to die for. Thank you for your precious blood that saved me. Thank you for the promise of heaven for eternity because I believe in you. Help me show my children and other moms how valuable they are to you, too. Amen.

I Don't Have to Have Everything Perfect

" The Lord does not look at the things man looks at. People look at the outward appearance, but the Lord looks at the heart."
1 Samuel 16:7

Have you ever compared yourself to another mom to gauge your own parenting success? We all do it. There is always the one who seems to have everything perfect. They always look put together, never frazzled. They participate actively in every PTA, room mom role, fundraiser, and yearbook committee that's offered. They juggle multiple kids in multiple sports and never seem to break a sweat. It doesn't seem fair.

If you somehow get past the mom who is involved in everything, you have the ones who are always dressed cute, with hairstyles that look straight from the salon, nails done, and makeup perfect. You run into a store, hoping you don't see anyone you know because you will never be that other mom.

I am so thankful for this verse in 1 Samuel 16:7. I don't have to do everything perfectly. I don't have to be completely put together. It's okay if I sometimes feel frazzled or I am running late from juggling multiple things. It's okay if my nails are chipped, my hair is in a messy bun, or I only wear tinted moisturizer and lip gloss. Don't judge. God doesn't.

People can look at my outward appearance all day long, but until they take the time to get to know me, they will never see my true heart. God does. I'm so glad God doesn't care about outward appearances.

Our worth is determined by God, not man. God looks at our inner hearts and sees beauty, compassion, love, and grace. He doesn't care what we are wearing or what committee we are on—He cares about our hearts.

Moment to Reflect:

- ♥ How does knowing God looks at the heart, not outward appearances, impact you? How does this change your view of yourself?
- ♥ Do you ever find you are comparing yourself to other moms (in appearance or involvement in kids/ classroom activities)?
- ♥ Do you measure your worth by how much you stack up to other moms?
- ♥ How can you help other moms feel more comfortable at school events, class parties, play dates, committee meetings, and other places moms may meet or get together?

It is hard to be a mom without adding the stress of feeling like you have to compete with other moms. We could all take a lesson from Jesus and try not to look at others through outward appearances. We are all just trying to do the best we can. Even if some look like they have it all together, we have no idea what they are going through behind the scenes. Thank goodness God looks at the heart.

Lord Jesus,

How many times have I compared myself to other moms? Help me to realize that my worth comes from you, and you don't look at outward appearances. Thank you for taking the time to look at my heart. Help me to build other moms up and encourage them because we are all just trying to be the best we can be for our kids. Amen.

What Truly Matters

"Don't be concerned about the outward beauty of fancy hairstyles, expensive jewelry, or beautiful clothes. You should clothe yourselves instead with the beauty that comes from within, the unfading beauty of a gentle and quiet spirit, which is so precious to God."
1 Peter 3:3-4 NLT

I am starting to notice a pattern regarding what God values and what truly matters, and it contradicts everything the world deems important. You should never question your worth because of a magazine with an edited photo of a model or a commercial with actors who have been styled by makeup artists.

What is Peter telling us in 1 Peter 3:3-4? He's not saying you can't wear makeup, nice clothes, or have your hair styled at the salon. He's saying if that's what you think makes you valuable, you're wrong.

This world puts value on appearance and material possessions to the point of exhaustion. Everywhere you look, there are billboards, ads, and magazines featuring models with the latest fashion or celebrities endorsing makeup brands. There are entire aisles and even entire stores dedicated solely to selling makeup and jewelry. This world is all about appearance. They care about the outside, which fades with time. Their value and worth are tied solely to superficial things.

God is much more interested in what's on the inside. He doesn't care about our outward appearance. Anyone can dress nicely and fix themselves up to play a part but be miserable on the inside. I can think of multiple times I have dressed up, applied makeup, fixed my hair, added jewelry, and went out in public smiling and acting like nothing was wrong when I was sad inside. But God knew. God knew when I would politely smile, but I was grieving my sister's death. God knew when I went through the motions of being okay but had recently miscarried and didn't want to talk.

God wants to know your heart and soul—the part of you that the world doesn't take time to get to know. He values your gentle and quiet spirit. He desires your heart to be pure, your words and actions to be gentle, and for you to promote peace. This was important to Him in Matthew 23:27-28 when He said, "Woe to you, teachers of the law and Pharisees, you hypocrites! You are like whitewashed tombs, which look beautiful on the outside but on the inside are full of the bones of the dead and everything unclean. In the same way, on the outside, you appear to people as righteous, but on the inside, you are full of hypocrisy and wickedness." If we invest everything in the outward and neglect our hearts, we cannot be an example of His love to others. When we are filled with the Holy Spirit and let Jesus lead our lives, His light shines through us, and no amount of makeup can make us more beautiful. When my kids see me, I want them to see a shine that powder cannot touch up. I want to be so close to Jesus that His light radiates from my eyes, and my smile is genuine because my joy comes from Him. Our kids need to know that Jesus matters to us in our lives. The gentle spirit you have when you let God's light shine through you is what shows Jesus to a world that needs to see beyond the superficial. When others see you, is your beauty only skin deep?

Moment to Reflect:

- ♥ Do you spend more time getting ready on the outside than you do with God to help change you on the inside?
- ♥ Do you put your worth in how you compare in appearance or style to the models in magazines and commercials?
- ♥ How can you change your mindset to value what is on the inside more? What are some ways you can encourage other moms to see their true beauty?

This world is so backward in how true beauty is measured. Everyone wants to look younger and prettier, and it can be exhausting trying to keep up with the latest trends. It's okay to take pride in your appearance, but don't ever let what is on the outside take precedence over what is on the inside. God cares more about the gentle way you respond to your kids or the kindness you show to another mom who is struggling than whether you look like you should be on the next cover of Vogue.

Lord Jesus,

I am only human, and I realize I have put too much emphasis on my appearance. Help me to crave you more and material possessions less. Help me to realize that true beauty comes from within and lights up a room. Help me to shine your light to others who need to see it. Thank you for loving me with or without makeup! Amen.

Our Weakness Makes Us Strong

But he said to me, "My grace is sufficient for you, for my power is made perfect in weakness." Therefore I will boast all the more gladly of my weaknesses, so that the power of Christ may rest upon me. For the sake of Christ, then I am content with weaknesses, insults, hardships, persecutions, and calamities. For when I am weak, then I am strong."
2 Corinthians 12:9-10 ESV

How many times have you stopped yourself from doing something or trying something because you didn't think you were strong enough or smart enough, athletic enough, or good enough? 2 Corinthians 12:9-10 tells me I don't have to be any of those things. It's okay to just be me. God doesn't see weakness as a stumbling block; He sees it as an opportunity to show His power. This is why it is important for us to be humble in our weakness rather than prideful. If we humbly submit to Him and allow Him to help us, others will see that there is no way we could have done these things on our own, and it points them to God.

We honor God more when we allow Him to work through our weakness with His strength rather than trying to handle our weakness by ourselves. Many times, we think we are not valuable to God because of our many weaknesses. Guess what? That is when God works best! I have often felt that I can't be valuable to God because I don't have one of those testimonies that stands out. But God can still use me as an encourager. He can use the experiences I have had and the lessons I have learned to speak the truth to moms who may need to hear it.

Paul wrote the book of Corinthians, and he dealt with something that he called a "thorn in his side." No one knows what it was, but he begged God to take it from him. God told him no, that His grace was sufficient. God continued to use Paul, and Paul even acknowledged that his weakness kept him from being conceited. He knew he had to rely on God to perfect his weakness.

When we have things we consider weaknesses in our lives, God looks and sees how He can sanctify us by stepping in and replacing that weakness with His power. I don't have to have a jaw-dropping testimony to be useful to God. God can take some of the trials I have gone through, the grief I have had to overcome, and the lessons I have learned just by being a mom, and He can use me to touch lives! When we go through hardships and difficulties, we should be relying on God for strength. Not only does He want to step in and help us, but when He does, others see that we aren't perfect, that we do need help, and that our Heavenly Father is there to fill the gap. He gets praise when we are weak because others realize there is no way we could have accomplished what we did or gotten through the difficulty without God. Our worth and value are not defined by worldly standards. God looks at us with all our flaws and our weaknesses, and He says, "I can use them. I want to make them strong."

Don't ever doubt your worth because of the difficulties and hardships you have. Every single hardship you have had to endure brought you to where you are now and made you who you are. Motherhood comes with hardships and difficulties. When we go through hard times as a mom, we don't need to crawl up into our tortoise shells and try not to be noticed. God knows where we struggle, and He wants to help us through it. When others know we have weaknesses, but they see us persevering anyway, God gets the glory. When our kids see we have weaknesses but we allow God to strengthen us, it helps them to see God can work in their lives, too. Consider yourself more valuable because you give God a reason to use His strength and power to perfect you, even in your weakness.

Moment to Reflect:

- ♥ Have you ever doubted your worth because of weaknesses in your life?
- ♥ Have you asked God to use you despite your weakness and give you strength through Him?
- ♥ Have you seen ways God has strengthened you when you knew you couldn't do it on your own? Allow Him to perfect His power in your weakness.

If you are a mom who feels that you have no worth because of a weakness or difficulty, ask God to strengthen you and perfect His power in your weakness. You are worthy. You are valuable to God. You have the opportunity to further His kingdom. By allowing Him to work through you despite your weaknesses, you bring glory to Him and show nonbelievers His true power at work. You are valuable as a mom, and you are valuable as a child of God.

Lord Jesus,

I have never felt truly worthy because I didn't think you could use me. I know I have weaknesses, but I pray that your grace will be sufficient for me. Use me in my life and let my children and others around me see your power through my weakness. Thank you for making me valuable in your kingdom. Amen.

You Are Valued

"And the very hairs on your head are all numbered. So don't be afraid; you are more valuable to God than a whole flock of sparrows."
Luke 12:7 NLT

D o you ever feel that in this great big world full of billions of people, you are insignificant? Do you ever question your worth or wonder if you have anything important to contribute to anyone? Do you feel valued? You should.

God, in all His infinite wisdom, created the sparrows and cares for them so much that not even a single one can fall to the ground without Him knowing (Matthew 10:29). Today's verse in Luke says we are more valuable than a whole flock of sparrows. If God cares enough to know when a single sparrow falls, a whole flock of sparrows would be even more important. This tells me I matter to God.

This verse about the sparrow is so important that there are songs written about it. I have a Christian playlist on my phone, and one of my favorite songs on my list is "His Eye is on the Sparrow" by JJ Heller. She sings that there is no reason for us to be dismayed and gloomy, feeling isolated and yearning for something more. If He can take care of a little bird, we should be confident He will take care of us.

God values you so much that He even knows the number of hairs on your head. Why would He care to know how many hairs you have if you weren't valuable to Him? He knows how many hairs you have because He cares about every detail of your life. You matter to Him. You matter so much to Him that He was willing to give His own son to die for us. Romans 5:8 says, "But God showed his great love for us by sending Christ to die for us while we were still sinners." No matter how good we are, we are all still sinners, but Jesus thought we were worth enough to die for. That makes me feel valued.

He made you just the way you are, and you are unique and special to Him. He wants to be included in every aspect of your life. What is important to you is important to Him. If it concerns you, He wants to help you have peace about it. When you struggle as a mom and feel like you don't measure up to other moms or you can't get it right, He wants you to know you are every bit as important as other moms. No mom is perfect.

You are special. You are loved. You are worthy.

Moment to Reflect:

- ♥ Do you struggle with your sense of worth?
- ♥ Do you have any idea how much God loves you, values you, and wants to be part of your life?
- ♥ When you hear a bird chirp or see one flying through the air, or when you brush your hair, stop and think about how much your God loves you and wants to be in your life.

Women are so hard on themselves, probably more than anyone else is. We judge ourselves, compare, and find fault with every aspect of ourselves. God doesn't want us to think that way. We matter to Him because He created us exactly how we are supposed to be. We aren't supposed to be a carbon copy of someone else. Know that your value comes from your Heavenly Father and not from the negative image you see yourself to be.

Lord Jesus,

I realize that my worth comes from you and no one else. You made me special, and I have a value beyond compare. Help me to turn to you when I struggle with my worth, and never forget that you know the number of hairs on my head and care about every detail of my life. I love you, Jesus. Amen.

Take A Second Glance

"For you created my inmost being; you knit me together in my mother's womb. I praise you because I am fearfully and wonderfully made; your works are wonderful;
I know that full well."
Psalm 139:13-14

When we look in the mirror, we often see our flaws and all the little things we don't like about ourselves. We may have a few extra creases around the eyes, or maybe our hair isn't the color or texture we would prefer. Maybe we see ourselves as too thin or not tall enough, or we're unhappy with our weight. We stare into this mirror, and our eyes are too small, or our nose is too big, and the list is just getting started!

Do you know what God sees? If you are ever standing in front of your mirror, and for some reason, you don't see the beautiful person God created staring back at you, you need to reread Psalm 139:13-14 and look at your reflection again. God knit you together perfectly, and you are a unique creation made by His hands. In case you missed the last part, the God of the Universe took the time to intricately weave you together in your mother's womb!

Think about that for just a second. Do you realize how special you are? God designed every part of you. The shape of your nose, the color of your eyes, the dimples in your chin, the color of your hair, and your personality were all created by God.

King David realized how special he was, and this is why he wrote these verses. He knew he was fearfully and wonderfully made, and he knew God did a good job. In Hebrew, "fearfully" is the word "yare," which means we were created with honor, reverence, and great respect. The word "wonderfully" in Hebrew is "pala," which means to be separate, distinguished, and unique. So, we are made uniquely special and created to have a reverent fear of God. Are you starting to feel better about yourself yet?

Go back and stand in front of your mirror. What do you see? You should see a masterpiece, fearfully and wonderfully made by the Creator of the Universe. Don't look for your flaws. Thank Him for your uniqueness, which makes you who you are. You are a reflection of Christ because you are made in the image of Him.

Moment to Reflect:

- ♥ Are you critical of yourself and your image?
- ♥ Take a moment and think about these verses in Psalms. Think about what it means to be created by Christ in His image.
- ♥ Ask God to help you see yourself as He sees you. Ask Him to help you reflect the love of Christ in everything you do.

Don't ever doubt that you are beautiful and special. God only creates masterpieces, and you are His unique creation.

Every part of you was designed by Him and for His plan for your life. Embrace who you are and thank God for fearfully and wonderfully making you.

Lord Jesus,

I am so critical of myself sometimes, and I'm sorry. You created me, and you made me special. Help me to see through your eyes the beauty you have created and be in awe that I was designed by the same God who created the Universe. I am fearfully and wonderfully made, and I am made in your image, so I must be special. Thank you for weaving me together and creating a plan for my life. Amen.

He Never Gives Up

"Being confident of this, that he who began a good work in you will carry it on to completion until the day of Christ Jesus."
Philippians 1:6

God isn't finished with us yet. He started a good work in us when we were saved, but He still has work to do. This promise that He will carry it on until the day of completion tells me that no matter how many mistakes I make, He will still be there. There will be areas where I struggle, but He will be there by my side to lift me up and show me the right way. He won't give up on me because He values me.

Have any of you ever started a project or began building something and never finished it? We have our kids' old baby bed that we want to turn into a bench for sentimental reasons, and it is not even halfway complete, sitting in our basement unfinished. We have multiple projects around the yard and house that need to be worked on, but we have put them off. We need trees dug up, a fence fixed, sod replaced, cabinets repainted, and the ceiling repaired, but we have not done a good job of carrying the work out to completion. These are all important, but we let other things get in the way. No matter how busy Jesus is, He is never so busy that He puts us aside! He continues to work on us until we join Him in eternity.

From the day we are saved, His Holy Spirit is constantly shaping us and molding us to become the person He wants us to be. As a Christian, my faith has grown through trials and hard times as I trusted Him to get me through. I have seen Him grow me in little ways as He helps me step out of my comfort zone and allow Him to move in my life. He continues to build our character and challenge us to try new areas of ministry and faith-based opportunities. When we step out in faith, we grow closer to Him because we rely on Him to provide where we know we can't. As moms, we begin teaching and shaping our children at an early age, and that carries on even into adulthood. We pray for them, root for them, discipline them, and love them no matter what. We don't give up on them just because they make mistakes along the way. Those mistakes help them learn, just like our mistakes help us learn and make better choices the next time.

God will continue working and drawing us closer to Him until Jesus comes back. We are being made into His image and should continually grow closer to Christ. So, if we are still breathing, He is working in our lives. It is comforting and encouraging to know that Jesus will work in my life until I see Him face to face. What does that do to your sense of worth to know Jesus will never give up on you and He is with you until the end?

If you are reading this and you don't have a personal relationship with Jesus yet, He is always waiting with open arms. It is never too late to trust in Christ. In the back of the book, there is a section on how to become a Christian. It just walks you through the process if you need some guidance. I encourage you to check it out if you have questions or you don't know how to proceed. Jesus loves you and wants to be part of your life.

Moment to Reflect:

♥ How does it make you feel to know that from the time you were saved, Jesus has been working in your life for your good?

♥ Do you have a past that made you doubt whether Jesus would truly stay and pour into your life until you see Him face to face?

♥ Are you growing in your walk with Him so He can mold you and shape you into who He wants you to be? If not, what changes can you make?

It makes me feel valued and loved to know that God will never give up on me. He will continue to work in my life to shape me into who I am supposed to become. I pray that I will help my kids feel as valued and worthy as God does.

Lord Jesus,

Thank you for beginning a good work in me and for staying with me until the end to complete it. I'm grateful for your promises and for the value you put on my life. Thank you for making me feel worthy even though I don't deserve it. I love you, Jesus. Amen!

Prayers For Your Child

"*I remember my mother's prayers and they have always followed me. They have clung to me all my life.*"
—Abraham Lincoln

Surrounded and Surrendered

"I have no greater joy than to hear that my children are walking in the truth."
3 John 1:4

As a Christian mom trying to raise my children to love Jesus and put Him first in their lives, today's verse rings so true for me. My main prayer every day for my kids is for all three of them to draw closer to Christ and seek Him in everything they do. This might seem like a cliché answer, but as I grow closer to Christ, I find that the things that once brought me joy now matter less. I still love to shop, read a good book, hike outdoors, watch love stories at Christmas, and eat ice cream. But, if I had to choose, there is no greater joy than my children walking close to God! We nurture them and guide them as they grow so that when they get to situations where hard choices must be made, they choose wisely. When they go through tough times, they hang on tight to Christ and let Him guide them.

I have seen my kids receive awards for leadership and academics, and I was very proud. I had a mom tell me my son helped her younger son at the gym, and it meant the world to me that he chose to be a good leader. I have had my daughter side with someone who had been left out just so that person wouldn't be alone. I have had other times when one of my kids didn't make the best choice, and there were consequences. The times that have made me the proudest were not awards for achievements and grades but the times that they showed the love of Christ to someone who needed it. As moms, all of us want to see our children grow in their faith and make good choices.

I know sports teams are important, as well as cheer, dance, soccer, music lessons, and other extracurricular activities, but even more important is seeing them living out the truth daily. If they are already believers, pray for them to listen to the Holy Spirit as He guides them. Pray for them to grow in their faith as they reflect the truth, grace, and love of Jesus in everything they do. Pray for them to surround themselves with Christian friends who will lift them up and encourage them in their faith. If they are not yet believers, pray for the Holy Spirit to speak to their hearts and for them to listen and surrender their hearts to Christ. Never stop praying for your children. My mom still prays for me, and I covet her prayers.

As their number one prayer warrior, teach them to pray. The disciples in Luke 11:1 said, "Lord, teach us to pray." Jesus teaches about prayer in Matthew 6: 5-12. He tells His disciples to pray alone, when possible, and pray sincerely instead of the same phrase over and over. He provides the Lord's Prayer as a model for our own prayers. Begin by honoring God, then ask Him for your needs and seek His forgiveness. Make requests for His assistance, and conclude by giving Him all honor and glory for who He is.

Moment to Reflect:

- ♥ Are you praying daily for your children to grow closer to Christ and for them to surround themselves with Godly influences?
- ♥ Is your child's walk with God more important than their extracurricular activities?
- ♥ Are there changes you can make to encourage your child to grow in their faith?

I pray daily for my kids, and some days, I feel like God is not listening at all. In my journey with God, I've noticed that when He appears silent, He is often working behind the scenes, making progress that I can't yet see. Don't ever doubt that He is listening. He works in His own timing and in His own way, and He has a plan. Trust it and trust Him to do amazing things in your child's life when you pray!

Lord Jesus,

My children are the most important gift you have given me. My prayer is that they know you and walk with you daily. Help them choose Godly friends who will lift them up and help them make good choices. I pray that your love and light will shine through me and that they will want that same light in their lives. Thank you for loving them and helping them walk in your truth. Amen!

Making a Difference for Christ

"I will give them a heart to know me, that I am the Lord. They will be my people, and I will be their God, for they will return to me with all their heart"
Jeremiah 24:7

We can pray for safety and write a list of rules for our kids to follow, but ultimately, the decision to walk justly and follow God is up to them. As moms, sometimes we can get wrapped up in all the ways we are protecting our children from harm, but their greatest danger could be their hearts' unwillingness to follow God.

We know as our children grow, they will have opinions of their own. While they are growing, we have the opportunity to pour into them the love of Christ and pray for them to have a life that is changed. They are going to make mistakes. They are going to face choices that go against God's standards. Our prayer for them should be that God is so real to them that their whole heart wants to obey Him. Pray that they won't settle for the world's ways but will desire to walk in truth.

How can we help them grasp for God instead of the sins that entice them? As moms, we can come boldly to the throne and pray for God to capture their hearts in such a way that they want to conform to God's standards and His will for their lives. Pray for their lives to be transformed so their choices honor Christ. When their choices don't honor Christ, pray that we will show grace and mercy to them. Sometimes, you learn grace and mercy and see the love of Christ even more when you fail. When we are able to model this for them, they see Christ in us. It's no different than how we want Jesus to handle us when we mess up!

Moms are a vital part of our children's lives. Our kids look to us for nurturing and love, and we can be a positive influence by our faith. Pray boldly for God to mold them into who He created them to be. Rules have their place, but I want my kids to make choices based on what God wants for them, not on what society says is correct.

Moment to Reflect:

- ♥ Do you place more emphasis on safety and rules than you do on your kids walking in truth?
- ♥ Are you praying for God to keep your child safe, or are you praying for God to change your child's life in a powerful way?
- ♥ If your children were outside of your home and your influence, would they make choices that would honor Christ? How can you pray boldly to ensure their hearts are changed?

We have such a powerful influence on our children, and we need to be sure we are using it for good. The sensible thing for any mom to do is to pray for the safety of her children, but sometimes, we need to step out in faith and let God take over. When our kids have hearts that are being molded and shaped into who God wants them to become, they will be in His hands, and that is the safest place any of us can be. Pray boldly!

Lord Jesus,

Thank you for my children and for letting me be their mom. I know the mom in me wants them safe, but help me to put them in your hands. I pray for them to be bold in their faith. As they leave the safety of my home for school or out with friends or as they go out into the world, help them to be so captivated by you that they choose to walk in truth always. Amen.

Stand in the Gap for Your Kids

"We demolish arguments and every pretension that sets itself up against the knowledge of God, and we take captive every thought to make it obedient to Christ."
2 Corinthians 10:5

Most children deal with anxiety at some point in their lives. This world is cruel, and school can be overwhelming for some. It's not just about trying to keep up with assignments, tests, and grades. It's the whole social aspect of friend groups, clubs, activities, and upperclassmen versus younger classmen. It's trying to fit in and not wanting to stand out. It's worrying about what others think and say.

Anxiety is real, and as your kids get older, they start to care more about what others think. There are bullies your child encounters on a daily basis who never lift a finger but can destroy your child with their words alone. Today's verse emphasizes the importance of spiritual warfare and how vital it is to take control of our thoughts. If we're not careful, our minds can become a gateway for Satan to gain a stronghold.

This verse also teaches us to reject worldly philosophies and ideas that oppose God's truth and instead align our values with Christ. By focusing on God's perspective and truth, we can overcome doubts, fears, and temptations.

Social media is also a huge aspect of anxiety for our kids. To reduce the anxiety from comparing and scrolling through the different accounts, limit their time on social media sites. In our home, one bedtime rule requires them to plug their phone or other devices into an outlet in a main area outside their room or in our room. The constant distractions from notifications or late-night scrolling hinder their sleep and increase the temptation to visit inappropriate sites. Try to have certain settings in place that are age-appropriate for your child. Use certain apps that can help to monitor your child and block them from inappropriate sites. Encourage them to have open conversations with us if they are struggling. Not only can we pray over them, but we can help tear down the lies of the enemy if we keep the conversation open. It may help to be transparent with them about our own struggles. Our kids need to know we need Jesus too!

This world is scary, and we need to stand in the gap for our children because Satan is trying to maneuver his way into every aspect of their lives. Pray this verse from 2 Corinthians over your child and help them to learn it and hide it in their heart. When they have a situation that makes them anxious, tell them to say this verse over and over to themselves and ask God to give them peace.

Moment to Reflect:

- ♥ Are you praying for your child daily and for their anxiety and anything they may be facing at school or practice or with friends?
- ♥ Have you taken measures to protect your child from inappropriate sites they could access through their phone? Are you separating them from their phone at night so you can better monitor what they have access to and let them get better sleep?
- ♥ Do you communicate openly with your kids and even with their friends' parents to find out what is going on at school, with friend groups, and with other kids? This is important to ensure they are okay.

Your child may be a talker and have great conversations with you about their day, but others may feel like you are pulling teeth to get even a one-word answer. I feel your pain. Stay strong, and don't ever quit praying for your children. They need your prayers, encouragement, and love.

Lord Jesus,

You have given me children to love and to nurture. Part of that love is knowing they are okay and knowing what is going on in their life. Help me to be aware of any stress in their life and help me to find ways to help alleviate it. Give me the courage to enforce rules regarding phones and social media because I know they can trigger even more stress. Help my kids realize everything I do is out of love. Help them to have the peace that can only come from you. I love you, Jesus. Amen.

Lighten Their Load

"Cast your cares on the Lord and he will sustain you; he will never let the righteous be shaken."
Psalm 55:22

This world seems much harder for kids than when I was little. Kids carry burdens these days that they shouldn't have to worry about. When they feel discouraged and face difficult situations, we don't need to worry about them going through it alone. Today's verse tells us that we don't have to carry our burdens alone. God doesn't want us to. He wants to help lighten our load. He can take the weight of the world on His shoulders, so allow Him to take your troubles from you.

Burdens are extra weight that drags us down and makes us tired. When the Psalmist says to cast your cares on the Lord, it literally means take your heavy load that is weighing you down and give it to Jesus. I picture my child with a heavy backpack that is weighing him down. It is overwhelming for him to walk one more step. Jesus comes along, knowing that my child is burdened and needs relief, so He takes the backpack and puts it on His own shoulders as He continues to walk beside him.

The burden is still there, but my child isn't having to handle it on his own.

How can you guide your child to give their burdens to God? There are some simple ways you can help them. One way is to let your children see you praying. When you are worried about something, share with your kids that you have concerns, but you are taking them to Jesus. Let them pray with you. You can also tell them about times God has given you peace after you prayed to Him. You can also sit down with them and go through some of the challenges they are facing and show them how to pray about what concerns them.

If you need a sample prayer to help you, you can modify this one:

"Dear God, I'm feeling [worried/sad]. I know you love me and want to help. Please take away my worry and give me peace. Help me trust you and remember you're always with me. Thank you for loving me and giving me peace. Amen."

It's important for your kids to talk to God just like they were talking to a friend. They don't need big words. You could set aside a certain time each day for them to pray so they can try to be consistent. I used to do bedtime prayers with my kids, but you could do them any time of day or a quiet moment when they are calm. When I taught Sunday School, we had a special jar or box, and they could write down any worries they had and put the piece of paper in the box. This was their way of giving their concerns to God.

By implementing some of these suggestions, you can help your child develop a personal prayer life and learn to give their burdens to God.

The Psalmist then says, "He will sustain you." This means He will support you. He will do anything within His power to support us and lift us up. Depending on what we are going through, our sustaining could be emotional, spiritual, or even physical. He can calm our emotions and give us peace. His Holy Spirit can speak to us spiritually and help us to feel closer to Him and less burdened. He can also heal us physically or reduce our stress to help us rest and feel better. The last part of the verse, "he will never let the righteous fall," means the righteous (the ones who love and fear God) will not be defeated. God will use His power to work in all situations and bring good from them to us who love and fear Him.

This simple verse packs so much into only a few words. They are more than words. They are promises of what God will do when we allow Him to take our burdens. Your kids don't have to struggle alone. They have you praying for them, and they have God who wants to lighten their load.

Moment to Reflect:

- ♥ Are your kids stressed out right now and seem to be burdened with the weight of the world?
- ♥ Do you feel helpless sometimes to know what to do to take away their stress and help them live life in abundance?
- ♥ Are you praying with passion and purpose for God to help carry their burden? He can do that for you, too. Sometimes, we allow the worry about our kids to weigh us down. Let Him lighten your load.

It is so hard when you see your child struggling. We want to take their problems away and we want to fix them. This world is cruel and hurtful, and growing up can be difficult. We can't always take away the stress and pain that can come through life. God isn't saying in this verse that He will take their troubles away and make everything perfect. He is saying that He will walk along beside them, and when the burden gets too heavy for them to handle, He will take the heaviness and carry it on

His shoulders as He continues to walk beside them through their tough times. The burden is still there, but they aren't alone in dealing with it.

Lord Jesus,

You love my children even more than I do, which is hard for me to imagine. I don't know what to do sometimes when they are hurting, stressed, or scared. Thank you for the promises in your word that give me comfort. Let me know you will be there to carry their burdens when they get too heavy for them to handle. I love you, Jesus. Amen.

Sever the Strongholds with Prayer

"Be alert and of sober mind. Your enemy, the devil prowls around like a roaring lion looking for someone to devour."
1 Peter 5:8

Imagine standing outside and scanning your fenced backyard, searching for the bobcat someone spotted in the woods near your house. Meanwhile, your tiny 6-pound dog remains oblivious to any danger.

The devil is that bobcat, and your child is that 6-pound dog. We need to pray 1 Peter 5:8 over our children because it paints a picture of Satan and how he is ready and willing to destroy our kids when they let down their guard. Even if our children are saved, Satan can still destroy their testimony and their ability to witness for Christ.

He's not just the bobcat. He's the pop artist with curse words and suggestive lyrics. He's the actor in the movie with the inappropriate scenes. He's the older kid who is offering your child substances he/she shouldn't have. Our kids need to pray for self-control because Satan is constantly tempting them in every aspect of their lives. They are automatically a threat to him just by being a Christian. He knows he can't take their eternity away, but if he can destroy their witness, he will use the lack of self-control to tempt them and cause them to ruin their testimony for Christ.

They can be alert by staying in God's Word and surrounding themselves with Godly friends who can encourage them in their faith and strengthen their walk with Christ. They need to be aware that temptation can come slowly in the form of gray areas and worm its way into their lives until Christ is the furthest thing from their minds. Their choices of shows and movies they watch, what they listen to, who they hang out with, and what they scroll through on their phones all play a part in how Satan chooses to devour them one step at a time.

As moms, we need to be vigilant in our prayer lives and never stop praying for our children. We can be alert and aware and pray for that hedge of protection around them so the devil can't get a stronghold. Don't ever think prayers don't matter. They are our lifeline to Jesus, and He hears every one of them.

Moment to Reflect:

- ♥ Do you pray for a hedge of protection around your children daily?
- ♥ Have you talked to your kids about the importance of self-control and staying alert when it comes to the temptations of Satan?
- ♥ Pray specifically for your child's friends. Pray that they have Godly influences in their lives that will strengthen them in their faith and encourage their walk with Christ.

We pray for our children to accept Christ, and we are so excited when they make that decision, but it doesn't stop there. They need to grow in their faith, make good choices, and make Godly friends so their faith will continue to grow. When they surround themselves with Godly influences, they have people to hold them accountable, to be self-controlled, and alert against the devil's temptations.

Lord Jesus,

Watch over my children and put your hedge of protection around them daily. Help them to be self-controlled and alert against the devil's schemes against them. Surround them with Godly influences that will lift them up and encourage them in their faith. Thank you for protecting them from the one who wants to destroy them. Amen.

Molded in the Mindset of Christ

"You were taught, with regard to your former way of life, to put off your old self, which is being corrupted by its deceitful desires; to be made new in the attitude of your minds; and to put on the new self, created to be like God in true righteousness and holiness."
Ephesians 4:22-24

In a world that has consistently excluded God, it is challenging for our kids to strive to live a godly life. Ephesians 4:22-24 acknowledges that we all need to abandon our old way of life before we were saved and cling to a new life with integrity and honor. Moms and children both need to seek God's help to become more like Him and less like the world. The number one difference between living for this world and living for God is selfishness. This world is sinful and selfish, and it encourages you to do whatever feels good to you regardless of who you hurt in the process.

When we release the distractions that hinder a life of honor and uprightness, we invite God to transform our thoughts, leading us to think of others, forgive, and live selflessly. It is a completely different mindset. As Christians, we aren't supposed to fit into the same mold as someone who has not accepted

Christ. Once we have Him in our hearts, His Holy Spirit leads and guides us, and we no longer have the same sinful desires.

This is a great verse for our kids to learn and hide in their hearts. As they grow older, their desire is to fit in and be like everyone else. When they conform to this world, the last thing they want to do is to be different. If you look up the word conform in a thesaurus, an actual synonym for it is "follow." As moms, the last thing we want is for our kids to follow the world's view. We want them to transform. We want them to be different than who they once were before Christ. When they open their minds to what God wants for them, their desires change to align with God's will. My desire for my children is for them to be at the center of God's will. This is my daily prayer for all three of my kids. They need a Godly mom praying this verse over them daily to help them resist Satan and his worldly temptations.

When we turn away from our old way of life, we allow our minds room for God to dwell, and then we will be able to discern God's will. His will is always what is best for us. This is why it is so important not to get caught up in what our culture says is best. If we are conforming to this world, we are showing God we love sin more than Him. We can't have it both ways. Ask God to give you the courage to be set apart and pray the same for your child.

Moment to Reflect:

- ♥ Are you living for this world or Christ? How do you know? What is the evidence of this in your life?
- ♥ Have you shared with your kids the subtle ways the world tries to lure them in? Talk about this and pray for your kids to be able to stand strong when others are conforming to what the world wants them to do.
- ♥ Pray specifically for your child to be bold in their faith. Pray for them to be surrounded by friends and Godly influences that will encourage them to live by God's will and not the world's standards.

Most of us don't want the spotlight on us as we go about our daily lives. Our kids are no different. They want to have friends, and they don't want to be ridiculed. Pray for them to have an influence and use it in a positive way for Christ. God puts each of them in certain groups and in situations to reach others for Him. Pray for them to know God's will and live it!

***

Lord Jesus,

My children need my prayers daily to live in this world and not conform to it. Help them to be bold in their faith and help them to live for you and not this world. Strengthen their faith and give them the integrity to face any situation with your help. Mold them into the Godly influences you want them to be instead of fitting into the mold the world wants them to conform to. Renew their minds and help them to know your perfect will for their lives. I love you, Jesus. Amen.

DAY 90

Captive for Christ

"'For I know the plans I have for you,' declares the Lord,
'plans to prosper you and not to harm you, plans to give you
hope and a future.'"
Jeremiah 29:11

How many of you have read today's verse and thought, "Not me"? God didn't get me out of that speeding ticket, God didn't stop me from getting in that bad relationship, or where was God when I lost my job, my spouse, my parent, my friend? I want to tell you that God was right there with you. You aren't a puppet He controls, and you have free will in the decisions you make. Sometimes, we make bad choices, and there are consequences. The Israelites figured that out when they were taken into captivity by the Babylonians. They had not been living according to God's will, and as a result, God allowed them to be captured by King Nebuchadnezzar and held in captivity for 70 years. This may seem harsh, but God did this because He loved the Israelites, and in this case, He had to demonstrate tough love.

As moms, we have to discipline our kids sometimes, even when we don't want to. They need to learn in order to grow. The Israelites strayed so far from God that they were not even worshiping Him anymore but idols instead. God tried to warn them first through prophets, but they didn't listen. How many times do we try to give our kids warnings before a punishment, and they don't stop their behavior? God is telling Jeremiah in today's verse that He has a better plan for them, even if it doesn't seem like it. His punishment was to wake them up and get their attention so they would turn back to God. God didn't allow the Israelites to stay in captivity forever. He restored them to their land and brought them out of captivity.

God's Word and His promises still apply to us today. He had a plan for them, just like He has a plan for us and our children. He doesn't always answer our prayers immediately or in the way that we may want Him to. The Israelites had to endure captivity for a season, but God was with them the entire time they were captured, and He gave them hope and a future in *His* timing.

So many of us are familiar with this verse or have even used it as a life verse for our children. His plans are never to harm us, but sometimes, the result of our sins can be painful and hard. He doesn't want that for us, but that is part of living in a corrupt world and having free will. God didn't make us puppets He can control. He allowed us to live free and make our own choices.

We need to pray for our children to make Godly choices and for them to honor Him in their thoughts and actions so their future will have hope and His plans for them will prosper. My prayer for my kids has always been for them to make Godly choices. There are going to be times when they mess up, and God reigns them in, but I have also seen times they have chosen to put God first, and it makes this momma's heart happy. They have led Bible study groups at church and been mentors to younger kids in the youth group. I have had one raise money on her own to go on a mission trip to another country. They don't have to lead in the limelight. Sometimes, making Godly choices means deciding against actions that could harm their reputation or future. I would rather their hearts be pure, and they lead behind the scenes away from the spotlight than draw attention to themselves and be prideful. It isn't a contest and doesn't have to be posted on Facebook or Instagram. When they are truly honoring God, their heart and their actions will show it.

How can they know God's purpose for their lives? They can seek Him and ask Him for wisdom and direction as they make decisions every day. They can ensure their thoughts are pure and let His Word and His Holy Spirit guide them. They can ask God to take their thoughts captive and make them obedient to Christ. They can obey His commandments, so they stay in fellowship with Him and feel His spirit nudging them in the right direction.

Today's verse is very uplifting, showing us God's plans to prosper us and give us a hopeful future. This is reassuring to me as a mother because I understand that there are occasions when I need to discipline my children. While they may not always appreciate it, I know it is always for their benefit. I need to be involved in their lives enough to know what they are listening to and watching and where discipline is needed.

God may discipline our kids as well, but He always has their best interests at heart. The Israelites were allowed to be captured by the Babylonians because they were not living right or making Godly choices. Pray for your child to make good choices that honor God. Ask the Lord to remind you of His faithfulness when your children are struggling with their own faith. Pray for His guidance to help you be a steadfast example of a devoted Christ follower, regardless of the circumstances.

Moment to Reflect:

♥ Are you praying for your child to surround himself with Godly friends and for their thoughts to be pure and their actions to be led by God?

♥ Do you know what your child watches, what songs and lyrics they listen to, and what games they play on a screen with others? What goes into your child's mind visually and audibly affects their actions. Monitoring the source can help eliminate bad influences on your child.

♥ Remember, Jeremiah 29:11 is a promise, but our kids must do their part by putting God first in their lives and honoring Him.

You have an opportunity to make a lasting impact on your children. Stay in tune with God by surrounding yourself with Godly moms, reading your Bible, soaking in the Scriptures, praising and worshiping your Savior, learning to trust God through your trials, and most of all, praying with all your heart for these precious children God has placed in your care. Don't ever underestimate the power of a Godly mom in a child's life. You truly do make a difference.

Lord Jesus,

Thank you for the promises of this verse and the hope they provide. Help me lift my children up to you and be involved in their lives to know what they are watching and listening to. I pray they are letting your Holy Spirit guide them so their choices will be in your will for their lives. Help them to always put you first and seek you as you direct them toward their future. Thank you for the blessing of being a mom. Help me never take for granted the impact I can have on the next generation. Amen.

How To Become A Christian:

ecoming a Christian is a personal decision that each of us has the choice to make. For some, the decision is made as a child, but for others, it is well into adulthood before they realize they need Jesus. If you feel led to invite Him into your heart, but you aren't exactly sure what to do, let me walk you through it.

We need Jesus because He is the bridge that helps us get to God. Let me explain. God created all of us in His image with the intention of being our friend and wanting us to experience an abundant life surrounded by His eternal love. John 10:10 confirms this when it says, "I have come that they may have life, and have it to the full."

God didn't make us puppets that He could control on a string or robots He could program. He gave us free will and allowed us the freedom to make our own choices. Unfortunately, we chose to disobey God, and this is when sin entered the world. None of us are perfect, and we all sin, and because of this, it creates a separation between us and God. Romans 3:23 says, "For all have sinned and fall short of the glory of God." God despises sin and can't be around it. **There is no way that we, by ourselves, can attain the perfection we need to bridge the gap to God.** We can't be good enough, smart enough, or rich enough to get into heaven.

Jesus Christ is our answer to help bridge the gap. God sent him to earth because, in biblical times, a sacrifice was needed to atone for sin. The people would sacrifice their perfect lambs, and that blood would cover the people's sins. When Jesus came, He lived a perfect life and willingly went to the cross as the ultimate sacrifice, dying to pay the penalty for our sins. He shed His blood so that we wouldn't have to. After three days, he rose again, conquering death. 1 Peter 3:18 says, "For Christ died for sins one for all, the righteous for the unrighteous, to bring you to God." Romans 5:8 also tells us, "But God demonstrates His own love for us in this; While we were still sinners, Christ died for us."

There are only two sides. There is the side of sin, rebellion, and separation from God, and there is the other side of peace, forgiveness, and abundant life with God. Which side are you on? John 3:16 tells us, **"For God so loved the world that He gave His one and only son, that whosoever believes in Him shall not perish but have eternal life."** He makes a promise in John 5:24, "I tell you the truth, whoever hears my word and believes Him who sent me has eternal life and will not be condemned; he has crossed over from death to life."

Now that you know the why, I want to tell you how you can become a Christian:

1. First, you need to admit that you are a sinner.
2. Then, be willing to repent and turn from your sins.
3. Next, believe that Jesus Christ died for you on the cross and rose again to conquer death.
4. Say a prayer and invite Jesus into your life and let His Holy Spirit live inside of you.

PRAYER:

Dear Jesus, I admit I am a sinner, and I need your forgiveness. I believe you died for my sins and rose again. I invite you into my heart and life. Help me to trust and follow you. In Your name, Amen.

If you prayed this prayer, congratulations! You are a Christian, and your eternity will be spent in Heaven with Jesus! All of Heaven rejoices when even one accepts Jesus as their savior. Find a friend and share the good news! Find a church home and get plugged in! Send me a message to my website, www.amybcrowe.com, so I can rejoice with you!

Sources

CHAPTER: ENCOURAGEMENT

Ball, Donna. *At Home on Ladybug Farm.* The Berkley Publishing Group, 2009.

CHAPTER: ANXIETY

Picoult, Jodi. *House Rules.* Atria Books, 2010.

Lucado, Max. *Traveling Light: Releasing the Burdens You Were Never Meant to Bear.* Thomas Nelson, 2001.

@katieinuganda. "Greek Word for Anxiety and What It Means." *Instagram*, 3 May 2024, www.instagram.com/p/C6aEkuiNpid/?igsh=ZHJubHl1eTFxc2ky.

Miller, Liz. *Fear Factors and Faith: Why Your Anxiety Doesn't Make You a Bad Christian.* Liz Miller Counseling, n.d. Web. 20 Aug. 2024. https://lizmillercounseling.com/fear-factors-and-faith-why-your-anxiety-doesnt-make-you-a-bad-christian.

"Anxiety Disorders." *National Institute of Mental Health*, U.S. Department of Health and Human Services, National Institutes of Health, n.d. Web. 20 Aug. 2024. https://www.nimh.nih.gov/health/topics/anxiety-disorders.

CHAPTER: STRENGTH

Biedert, Elena. "The Strength of a Mother." *Fit-Pro*, 10 May 2024, Personal Fitness Professional (PFP) -

CHAPTER: DIRECTION

Barry, Helen (@helenmbarry). "As your mother I promise you that I will always be..." *Instagram*, 24 July 2018, www.instagram.com/p/BlihasWgNQS/.

CHAPTER: WISDOM

Abdelnour, Ziad K. "Be strong enough to stand alone, smart enough to know when you need help, and brave enough to ask for it." *20 Quotes About Strength*, *The Healthy*, 24 Jan. 2024, www.thehealthy.com/mental-health/quotes-about-strength/.

Alexander, Max. *All About House Foundations. This Old House*, 24 July 2024, www.thisoldhouse.com/home-improvement/21015112/all-about-house-foundations. Accessed 20 Aug. 2024.

Bridge Media. "The Importance of a Quality Foundation." *GoliathTech Piles*, 9 May 2023, www.goliathtechpiles.com/the-importance-of-a-quality-foundation. Accessed 20 Aug. 2024.

CHAPTER: GOD'S WILL

Nicogossian, Clair. "10 Quotes on Motherhood Sure to Make You Smile." *Momswellbeing.com*, 7 May 2017, www.momswellbeing.com/10-quotes-motherhood-sure-make-smile/.

"Greek Lexicon Entry for 'Will' (θέλημα)." *Breakthrough Version*, n.d., www.breakthroughversion.com/greek/lexicon/will.

"Greek Lexicon Entry for 'Good' (ἀγαθός)." *Breakthrough Version*, n.d., https://www.breakthroughversion.com/greek/lexicon/good.

CHAPTER: FAITH

Ved. "A Mother's Love Knows No Bounds: 100+ Proud Mom Quotes!" *Wellness by VED*, 30 Mar. 2024, www.wellnessbyved.com/proud-mom-quotes/.

CHAPTER: EXAMPLE

Edwards, Sarra. "Quotes to Inspire You on the Hard Mom Days." *Sarraedwards.com*, 6 Jan. 2018, www.sarraedwards.com/blog/quotes-to-inspire-you-on-the-hard-mom-days.

CHAPTER: FRIENDSHIP

Kwan, Michael. "Sunday Snippet: Jill Churchill on Motherhood." *Beyond the Rhetoric*, 16 July 2017, www.btr.michaelkwan.com/2017/07/16/sunday-snippet-jill-churchill/.

CHAPTER: PEACE

Sykes, Logan, and Katie Robinson. "40 Mother's Day Quotes That Almost Express How Much You Love Your Mom." *Town & Country*, 7 Apr. 2022, www.townandcountrymag.com/leisure/arts-and-culture/news/g246/mothers-day-quotes/.

CHAPTER: PURPOSE

Campelli-Ignacz, Gabriella. "10 Beautiful Motherhood Quotes to Brighten Up Your Day." *Wellbeing for Mothers*, 14 Mar. 2019, www.wellbeingformothers.com/2019/03/14/10-beautiful-motherhood-quotes-to-brighten-up-your-day/.

CHAPTER: WORTH

Hanson, Kait. "30 Inspirational Mom Quotes to Lift Up All Mothers." *Today*, 13 Apr. 2023, www.today.com/parents/moms/inspirational-mom-quotes-rcna79195.

Devotion #82

Hall, Tessa Emily. "How Can We Know We're 'Fearfully and Wonderfully Made'?" *iBelieve*, 2 June 2022, www.ibelieve.com/faith/how-can-we-know-were-fearfully-and-wonderfully-made.html.

CHAPTER: PRAYERS FOR YOUR CHILD

Matsoso, Ally. "A Prayer to Notice." *Philosophy of Motherhood*, 19 Aug. 2020, www.philosophyofmotherhood.wordpress.com/2020/08/19/on-prayer/.

Acknowledgments

I want to thank my husband, who has always encouraged me to pursue my dreams. He has been patient with the long hours I've spent pouring into my writing, and his support has uplifted me and made me feel equipped when I felt inadequate. I couldn't have done this without him.

Special thanks to Abby McDonald, my developmental editor, who was always gracious and affirming with my manuscript. Her constructive editing transformed my original draft into a work I am proud of. I am grateful for her expertise and for getting to know her kind spirit throughout the process.

I want to thank Krissy Nelson for believing in me and bringing me to hope*books and Brian Dixon for his leadership. I also extend my thanks to everyone at hope*books for their commitment to being a Christian publisher. hope*books provides weekly calls, coaching, and guidance through its system, helping us stay on track and connect with the support we need at each stage of the publishing process. They genuinely care about the author and the message each book aims to share.

I also want to recognize my hope*books May 2023 Cohort. This group of talented individuals has formed a special bond during our time at hope*books. We meet weekly, cheer each other on, provide information and support, and have become like family. This camaraderie has been an integral part of my publishing journey, and the relationships and friendships we've formed will last long after my book is released.

Lastly, I want to thank you, my reader. Thank you for choosing this book and allowing its message to guide you in your faith journey. My hope and prayer are that this message resonates with you and that you can apply what you've learned to your own life. I hope you know through all the words I've written that you are important to God. You have unique gifts and abilities that can help others. You have a purpose in this life. You matter.

About The Author

Hi, I'm Amy Crowe, a craft-loving mom of three and the lucky wife of Brad. I'm a writer, crafter, amateur artist, and a cheerleader for all moms out there. My family and I call Birmingham, Alabama home, where we share our space with a lively Golden Retriever and a sassy Maltese, who keep things interesting.

When I'm not immersed in writing, you'll find me in my craft room, diving into new projects for my craft business. I love escaping into a good book, exploring the great outdoors on hikes, and enjoying walks or lunch dates with friends. Whether it's the beach or the mountains, I cherish every moment spent in nature.

Being a mom is my greatest joy and calling, and I'm deeply passionate about supporting and encouraging other moms in this vital role.